Routledge Author Guides

Southey

Routledge Author Guides

GENERAL EDITOR: B. C. SOUTHAM, M.A., B.LITT. (OXON)
Formerly Department of English, Westfield College, University of London

Titles in the series

Browning by Roy E. Gridley

Byron by J. D. Jump

William Cobbett by James Sambrook

Macaulay by Jane Millgate

J. S. Mill by Alan Ryan

Nietzsche by R. J. Hollingdale

Southey by Kenneth Curry

Tolstoy by Ernest J. Simmons

Routledge Author Guides

Southey

by

Kenneth Curry

Professor of English
University of Tennessee, Knoxville

Routledge & Kegan Paul
London and Boston

First published in 1975
by Routledge & Kegan Paul Ltd
Broadway House, 68–74 Carter Lane,
London EC4V 5EL and
9 Park Street,
Boston, Mass. 02108, USA
Set in Bembo
and printed in Great Britain by
Cox & Wyman Ltd, London, Fakenham and Reading

ISBN 0 7100 8112 X

*To Bain Tate Stewart
colleague and friend*

General Editor's Preface

Nowadays there is a growing awareness that the specialist areas have much to offer and much to learn from one another. The student of history, for example, is becoming increasingly aware of the value that literature can have in the understanding of the past; equally, the student of literature is turning more and more to the historians for illumination of his area of special interest, and of course philosophy, political science, sociology, and other disciplines have much to give him.

What we are trying to do in the Routledge *Author Guides* is to offer this illumination and communication by providing for non-specialist readers, whether students or the interested general public, a clear and systematic account of the life and times and works of the major writers and thinkers across a wide range of disciplines. Where the *Author Guides* may be seen to differ from other, apparently similar, series, is in its historical emphasis, which will be particularly evident in the treatment of the great literary writers, where we are trying to establish, in so far as this can be done, the social and historical context of the writer's life and times, and the cultural and intellectual tradition in which he stands, always remembering that critical and interpretative principles are implicit to any sound historical approach.

BCS

Contents

Contents

Preface

The purpose of this volume on Southey in the Routledge Author Guides is to introduce Southey to the reader who has no special knowledge or acquaintance with him, either in his biography or in his works, and who may not even have any special knowledge of the literature, the history, or the social and political conditions of the years at the beginning of the nineteenth century. I have not endeavored to be encyclopedic in treating either his life or his works, nor have I tried to introduce new material or to produce original readings of his many works. I have tried rather to present his career and his works in a favorable light in terms of the difficulties of his own life as a professional man of letters and in the very confusing times in which he lived, a time in many ways not unlike the present with its wars, revolutions, threats of social disruption, and its threats to old established institutions and mores.

The notes are for the most part incorporated within the text and a table of abbreviations on p. xii gives the list of those works most frequently cited. A Bibliography at the end of the book provides the reader with a list of the standard editions of Southey's works, useful selections, and important books and articles.

Abbreviations

Bowles	*The Correspondence of Robert Southey with Caroline Bowles*, ed. Edward Dowden, Dublin, 1881.
Carnall	Geoffrey Carnall, *Robert Southey and His Age*, Oxford, 1960.
CPB	Southey's *Common-Place Book*, ed. J. W. Warter, 4 vols, London, 1849–51.
Letters	*Selections from the Letters of Robert Southey*, ed. J. W. Warter, 4 vols, London, 1856.
Letters of Scott	*The Letters of Sir Walter Scott*, ed. H. J. C. Grierson, 12 vols, London, 1932–7.
Life	*The Life and Correspondence of the Late Robert Southey*, ed. C. C. Southey, 6 vols, London, 1849–50.
New Letters	*New Letters of Robert Southey*, ed. Kenneth Curry, 2 vols, New York, 1965.
Reminiscences	Joseph Cottle, *Reminiscences of Samuel Taylor Coleridge and Robert Southey*, London, 1847.

Part I

Robert Southey:
His Life, His Age,
His Literary Friends

I

1774-1795

Boyhood and Youth

Robert Southey was born on August 12, 1774, in Bristol, the oldest surviving child of Robert and Margaret Hill Southey. His father, the son of Somerset farmers, had been apprenticed to a linen-draper, and at the time of his marriage in 1772 was proprietor (with his brother Thomas) of his own shop in Wine Street. The father's real interests, unfortunately for his financial well-being, were not in shop-keeping, but rather in rural pursuits and field sports: the sign of his shop was that of a hare. 'The fields,' as his son phrased it, 'should have been his station, instead of the shop' (*Life*, vol. 1, p. 7). Of the nine children born to the Southeys only four – Robert, Thomas, Henry Herbert, and Edward – lived to maturity, the others dying in infancy or early childhood. From two until six Robert lived, not with his parents in Bristol, but in Bath, where his mother's half-sister, the beautiful, eccentric, and violent-tempered Miss Elizabeth Tyler, had a house. Through her imperious personality and the power of her purse Miss Tyler dominated Mrs Southey, who was twelve years her junior. Although by no means rich, Miss Tyler lived ostentatiously, had a large acquaintance, and went out almost every night. The series of vivid autobiographical letters which Southey wrote in the 1820s recall innumerable details of Miss Tyler's household, her friends, and her style of living; by contrast, the letters tell us almost nothing of his father's home in Wine Street. The theater was Miss Tyler's special interest, and Southey remembered attending his first play – Henry Fielding's *The Fathers* – at the age of four.

This household of Miss Tyler was in no way suited to a child. Forced to sleep in her bed and to remain perfectly quiet until she chose to arise at nine or ten, 'my poor little wits were upon the alert . . .

fancying figures and combinations of forms in the curtains, wondering at the motes in the slant sunbeam.' Miss Tyler, moreover, had a passion for cleanliness, and devised such childhood games as pricking playbills with a pin and cutting fantastic figures from paper.

At the age of six, Southey was removed from Miss Tyler's house and lived at his father's in Bristol in order to attend Mr Foot's school as a day-pupil, where he was bullied by both master and students. The next year his parents enrolled him at a school at Corston, a village nine miles from Bristol. Housed in an old mansion, Southey described it in 'The Retrospect':

> Large was the house, though fallen, in course of fate,
> From its old grandeur and manorial state . . . .
> There now in petty empire o'er the school
> The mighty master held despotic rule;
> Trembling in silence all his deeds we saw,
> His look a mandate, and his word a law;
> Severe his voice, severe and stern his mien.

Thomas Flower, the master of the school, was interested chiefly in mathematics and astronomy, but writing and arithmetic were taught, and twice a week a Frenchman came to teach Latin. One feature of the school life in which Southey excelled was the spelling match on which the students placed bets. Flower himself was ineffectual, his wife had taken to drink, and when the itch broke out among the students, all the Bristol boys were withdrawn from the school. 'There could not be a worse school in all respects' (*Life*, vol. 1, p. 48), Southey later judged.

A Welshman, William Williams, conducted the school which Southey attended for the next four or five years, and although this experience proved pleasant enough, the studies were neither rigorous nor demanding. An usher taught Latin, but Williams himself taught writing, arithmetic, merchants' accounts, and examined the students in the Catechism. At Williams's school Southey learned that he could compose rhymes. Vacations during this period were spent either with Miss Tyler and her friends or at his grandmother's house at Bedminster. Having given up her house in Bath, Miss Tyler was then living with Miss Palmer and Mrs Bartlett, who as part owners of the Bristol and Bath theaters lived adjacent to the theater at Bath. There they all went – young Robert included – almost every evening. The theater became his introduction to Shakespeare and to history: 'It was

4

long before I had any other knowledge of the history of England than what I gathered from his plays' (*Life*, vol. 1, p. 70). The theater at Bath at this time had truly fine performances with Sarah Siddons as the leading lady: '. . . . it is impossible to describe the thorough delight which I received from this habitual indulgence . . . I saw it in perfect comfort, in a small theatre, from the front row of a box, not too far from the centre' (*Life*, vol. 1, p. 72). This familiarity with the stage and plays led to thoughts of writing for the theater. 'It is the easiest thing in the world to write a play!' he once informed Miss Palmer, 'for you know you have only to think what you would say if you were in the place of the characters, and make them say it.' On returning to Williams's school after the vacation, Southey encouraged two of his fellow-students to write plays but without success, and he himself found it harder to do than he had first thought and abandoned the project after completing an act and a half. Southey remained at Williams's for four or five years until he was about twelve, living at home at his father's or later with Miss Tyler after she took a house in Bristol on Teril Street. These years passed on the whole very pleasantly: 'Of all my schoolmasters Williams is the one whom I remember with the kindliest feelings' (*Life*, vol. 1, p. 94). But the school was deteriorating both in numbers and in quality, and Southey was removed.

At this point in Southey's life, his maternal uncle, the Reverend Herbert Hill, who was the chaplain to the British residents at Oporto and Lisbon, made the first of several decisions which were to give direction to his life. Educated at Christ Church, Oxford, and the owner of a small estate in Herefordshire, Mr Hill took the place that Southey's own father had abdicated under the pressures of his strong-willed sister-in-law. The plan was to provide for the young Robert by sending him to Westminster School, from thence to Christ Church, and when safely in holy orders, to be provided by a living within the gift of Mr Hill. That the plan did not work exactly as sketched does not detract a whit from the generous foresight of the uncle in his attempt to provide for his nephew, who was early showing gifts for writing and study.

The poor quality of Southey's schooling resulted in his being placed, early in 1787, with a clergyman named Lewis, who instructed a few pupils during the morning between ten and two. This instruction was designed to prepare him for Westminster School, but Southey remembered only that 'I began Greek under him, made nonsense-verses, read the *Electa ex Ovidio et Tibullo* and Horace's Odes, advanced a little in writing Latin, and composed English themes.'

Southey's reading began early in life, and he devoured the entire set of children's books published by Thomas Newberry, whose son (a friend of Miss Tyler and member of her circle) had given them to him. His next discovery was Hoole's translation of Tasso's *Jerusalem Delivered*, a book still in his possession in 1823 and even then 'in excellent preservation considering that when a schoolboy I perused it so often that I had no small portion of it by heart' (*Life*, vol. 1, p. 83). Not only Tasso, but also Ariosto's *Orlando Furioso* was a favorite. To Hoole's work as translator Southey recorded his indebtedness: 'the translator rendered me a service which . . . I cannot estimate too highly. I owe him much also for introducing me to Spenser' of whose work he learned in one of Hoole's notes. Acting on this information Southey sought the work at Bull's circulating library at Bath. 'No young lady of the present generation falls to a new novel of Sir Walter Scott with keener relish than I did that morning to the Faery Queen' (*Life*, vol. 1, p. 65). From Spenser he went to Chaucer, Percy's *Reliques*, and then to Homer and the Bible. The popular poets of the day – Gray, Collins, Cowper, Mason, Warton, Akenside – served as models for much of his juvenile poetry.

Southey's schooling at Westminster and the friendships he formed there were a most significant and formative influence in his life. His highly irregular education in makeshift schools conducted by incompetent schoolmasters had not prepared him for the traditional and rigorous classical training which formed the curriculum at Westminster. The saving feature of this poor education was a leisure which he had employed in reading. Much of Southey's education seems to have been self-education and self-motivated. It is indeed difficult to discover from what external source he derived the impetus towards reading, study, and writing. 'I do not remember,' he later recorded, 'in any part of my life to have been so conscious of intellectual improvement as I was during the year and half before I was placed at Westminster; an improvement derived, not from books or instruction, but from constantly exercising myself in English verse.' The lack of a regular home life and the long periods of residence in the eccentric household of Miss Tyler could have damaged his personal development, but he seems to have been remarkably resilient and responded to whatever the situation demanded. At times he lacked the society of his contemporaries, but there were always fellow-students at the day schools he attended and the boarding school at Corston. His brother Tom was only three years younger, and Miss Tyler's servant Shadrach Weeks, sister of her maid, was exactly of an age with Southey, and proved a congenial companion for country rambles and for elaborate exercises in carpentry, one of which led to the construction of a small theater for puppets. Throughout his life Southey enjoyed human companionship and was always surrounded with congenial associates. Despite his love for reading and his facility with the pen and the solitariness that necessarily accompanies those pursuits, he was never a recluse.

Westminster and Eton were the two leading public schools of the day, and Westminster with its 260 students provided the best education available to a boy enrolling in 1788. The curriculum was strictly classical, based upon Latin and Greek. Great emphasis was placed upon writing in Latin and in composing Latin verses. Southey chafed under this compulsion to produce Latin verses, and in one of his earliest letters – a verse epistle to his Westminster schoolfellow Charles Collins – he strongly asserts the superiority of English to Latin verse.

> Yet still my native tongue demands my lays
> And there and there alone I seek for praise.
> Let not thy once lovd friends request be vain
> Write soon in verse and English be the strain.
>
> (*New Letters*, vol. 1, p. 3)

The students at Westminster lived in boarding houses near the school. Southey lived at Ottley's – under the nominal supervision of Samuel 'Botch' Hayes, an assistant master whose nickname derived from his correction of the students' verses. The head of the house, Lord Amherst, an amiable boy who lived to himself in a room of his own, did not enforce discipline, and the result was that during the year Southey suffered his share of school tyranny. The most frightening experience was to be held by the leg out of the window – 'had I not struggled in time, and clung to the frame with both hands, my life would probably have been sacrificed to this freak of temporary madness.' The two most dangerous boys – William Forrester and Robert Brice – hated each other and vented some of their maliciousness on each other, but Forrester, who was inept in his studies, forced the younger boys to do his Latin exercises for him, Southey finally being promoted to the honor. 'My orders were that the exercises must

7

always be bad enough; and bad enough they were: I believe, indeed, that the habit of writing bad Latin for him spoilt me for writing it well, when, in process of time, I had exercises of the same kind to compose in my own person' (*Life*, vol. 1, p. 151). The reminiscences of Southey concerning Westminster do not dwell upon these misfortunes or incidents of school tyranny – nor indeed upon the subjects taught – but rather upon his fellow students with brief glances at the various masters. At the time of Southey's entrance, Samuel Smith was the headmaster to be succeeded during his first year by the Under-Master, William Vincent, a scholar whose specialty was ancient geography. Southey's first teacher, Edward Smedley, the tutor of the fourth form, was kindly and did Southey the initial good service of selecting George Strachey to be Southey's substance. The Westminster custom was to assign an older boy, who was called the substance, to the new boy, denominated the shadow, and whose task it was to initiate the newcomer into the habits and customs of the school. 'Strachey and I were friends at first sight,' Southey recorded, and since Strachey lived at home, the Strachey home on Queen Anne Street became one of the houses in which Southey was welcome during these student days. The sonnet, 'Fair be thy fortunes in the distant land,' is Southey's poetic tribute to George Strachey, who left England for a distinguished career in India. There is evidence that Southey had his share in the usual schoolboy mischief. He himself tells one story of joining a group of Westminsters who were bent on harassing or 'beating up' the quarters of a small school in a house near St Margaret's churchyard, and provoking the master. 'The sport was to see him sally with a cane in his hand, and to witness the admiration of his own subjects at our audacity.' A complaint to Dr Vincent brought an end to the business, but the real culprits were never discovered. Southey's curly head almost brought him into trouble because the schoolmaster, unable to identify any of the assailants, could only state that one of the boys had a curly head, which brought another curly-headed youth to a questioning. Charles Lamb reported years after that Southey had also had his share in mutilating the nose of the statue of Major André. In November, 1791 a school rebellion took place in which two boys fought over a piece of ribbon. Years later Southey still had a piece of this ribbon as a token of the struggle, and admitted (*Life*, vol. 4, p. 319) that he had had his share in this school rebellion – one celebrated enough to be written up in the newspapers.

It was not, however, in these minor and relatively unimportant aspects of school life that Westminster had its greatest impact on Southey. It was rather in the friendships that he formed there. The two deepest and most abiding were with Charles Watkin Williams Wynn, second son of a baronet and nephew of Lord Grenville, and Grosvenor Charles Bedford, son of Horace Walpole's substitute as Deputy Usher of the Exchequer. These lifelong friendships were marked by the exchange of letters for over forty years. Because of his position in the world, Wynn was able to be of considerable service to Southey, his chief act being the grant of a pension of £160 to Southey in the year 1797. This generous act was doubly so because Wynn, despite his rank in the Whig oligarchy, was not a rich man. His general outlook was essentially conservative in literature as well as in politics, and Southey at no time in his life can ever be said to have shared in any complete way the political positions to which Wynn adhered. Bedford was in some ways more congenial and similar to Southey. Their position in society was quite firmly middle class, and temperamentally, they shared a fondness for humor and puns. Bedford also shared Southey's zeal for writing, and his bibliography, although not voluminous, is substantial. A writer of many poems and several pamphlets, he also reviewed for the *Quarterly*. He appears not to have shared Southey's revolutionary enthusiasms, to have been rather sceptical of utopian dreams, and to have been perfectly content to follow the routine of a reliable, hard-working clerk at the Exchequer, who by dint of good work and years of faithful service would be rewarded by small increases in salary and responsibility. But at the time of his school friendship with Southey, and for many years thereafter, he enjoyed dreams of modest literary fame, as well as the association with literary and educated men (William Gifford was another literary friend). In 1820 Southey wrote: 'You are my only *frequent* and constant correspondent, the only person, with whom correspondence has become a habit; with whom I can be grave or nonsensical, to whom I can say quidlibet de quolibet [all and everything from wherever it comes], and make my lightest thoughts legible as they rise' (*Letters*, vol. 3, p. 212).

In addition to these two special friends, a host of others could be mentioned. With many of the Westminster boys he was on sufficiently friendly terms to be invited to their homes – since Southey really had no home of his own to go to during vacations these invitations were not unimportant for him. The Strachey house in London was one where he was welcome, and that of Thomas Davis Lambe of Rye was another. The most distinguished person – apart from Wynn – who became Southey's friend was Peter Elmsley, the classical scholar and archaeologist, but the loss of their correspondence makes it difficult to estimate their intimacy. Most of his school friendships did not outlast the schooldays, but Westminster was the experience to which Southey always referred for the rest of his life, and of which he occasionally dreamed. Old Westminsters often came as visitors to the Lake District, and were always made welcome at Greta Hall. Letter after letter contains allusions to fellow-students, often grief and disappointment at their failures and early deaths – a very large number of his contemporaries at school joined the army or navy and died on distant stations and battlefields from the West Indies to Africa.

But the pleasant days at Westminster were not to end on a joyous note. Mr Hill had hoped that Southey would be entered at Christ Church College, where his friendship with Dr Cyril Jackson, the dean, might be helpful in getting Southey on the foundation. During the winter of 1792 Southey, together with Wynn, Bedford, and Strachey, planned a school paper modeled upon the successful Eton publication, *The Microcosm* (1787). Wynn and Strachey left school before the paper appeared so that all nine numbers were written by Bedford and Southey. The work was entitled *The Flagellant,* and the originators assumed such fanciful titles as St Peter the Hermit (Bedford), St Pardulph (Wynn), St Basil and Gualbertus (both names for Southey). The work appeared weekly from March 1 to April 26, 1792, but the fifth number, devoted to an article on flogging, contained the argument that corporal punishment had no place in a Christian school since it was the work of Satan. Dr Vincent, the headmaster, had no difficulty in discovering the author, promptly expelled Southey, and warned Cyril Jackson about the dangers of admitting such a young rebel. Southey was naturally stunned and upset, and his letters reveal his sense of injustice, together with a certain amount of self-pity. Dr Vincent appears to have acted with an undue severity, and there is the suspicion that he may have welcomed the chance to pay off some old scores. Ten years later Southey recalled the incident and Vincent's role thus: 'I was to blame – but less than he was, the punishment exceeded the offence, and Vincent never used me well – because I was the son of a country tradesman. This was less felt by me than it was seen by others – but there were palpable and shameful instances – for I was perhaps the most regular in my conduct of all who were under him' (*New Letters*, vol. 1, pp. 293–4). This instance of snobbery was not the only one which Southey suffered during his youth, but he seemed to have been indifferent to these slights and scarcely mentioned them.

The Age of Revolution

POLITICS AND WAR

Southey was born into a world of revolution and change. Two years after his birth the American Revolution broke out, and when he was fifteen the French Revolution began in 1789. The period from his birth until 1832 saw the emergence of the United States (a government that did not need a monarch, a nobility, or an Established Church), the French Revolution and the rise of Napoleon, the ultimate defeat of Napoleon and France, and the passing of a series of reform measures from an extension of the franchise to a modest reform of the legal code. In addition to these dynastic and political changes in Europe, there were new ideals of equalitarianism, democracy, and a spirit of national identity accompanied by a change from an agricultural to an industrial economy. Today a rapid degree of social and economic change is accepted as a natural thing, but to those living in the eighteenth century these changes were something new and to many terrifying. Young men such as Southey and Wordsworth, however, welcomed them. A new day seemed to be dawning. 'Few persons,' Southey recalled, 'but those who have lived in it can conceive or comprehend what the memory of the French Revolution was, nor what a visionary world seemed to open upon those who were just entering it. Old things seemed passing away, and nothing was dreamt of but the regeneration of the human race' (Bowles, p. 52). If such high hopes were not quite realized, the new age was to bring many changes. Old barriers of class and position were weakened, if not abolished, and the energies of the individual had new scope for exercise and fulfilment.

The reactions to the Revolution were varied and changed with the events. During the six years from 1789 to 1795 – from Southey's fifteenth to twenty-first year – Southey, like many, many others, welcomed the Revolution as offering a new hope for man. Those with a deep commitment to the underlying beliefs and hopes retained their faith and found excuses or overlooked the violence and bloodshed in Paris and the victories of the French on the battlefield. During these early years there is no doubt that Southey and Coleridge held firmly to the faith in all the best that the Revolution stood for; it was not until later in the decade that the conquests throughout Europe and the ruthless aggression of Bonaparte made them and others turn away. Not all those who welcomed the Revolution were young, radical, and poor. Charles James Fox, leader of the governmental opposition, had kind words for the Revolution. A group of prominent Whigs including Charles Grey (later a prime minister), Erskine, Sheridan, Lord Edward Fitzgerald, and the wealthy brewer Samuel Whitbread formed a club, entitled The Friends of the People, in April of 1792. Many other societies were formed, often of small numbers and of short duration. Dissenting ministers and well-to-do, well-educated dissenters were often the mainstay of some of these organizations. At first, the working classes were not represented among those who sought or agitated or wrote for reforms on the French model.

The official position of the government was one of restraint. William Pitt, the prime minister, hoped that the French would settle their internal affairs upon a sensible basis. But others were not so hopeful. Edmund Burke was one of these, and in a series of speeches and in his famous and widely read pamphlet *Reflections on the Revolution in France* (1790) he sought by every force of eloquence at his command to arouse the public to the danger. The basis of his argument was a conservative one that any change in the existing arrangements would be disastrous to the fabric of society. 'The equilibrium of the Constitution has something so delicate about it, that the least displacement may destroy it.' The changes that the French had sought were a profound object lesson to all for they 'have shown themselves the ablest architects of ruin who have hitherto existed in the world. In a short space of time they have pulled to the ground their army, their navy, their commerce, their arts, and their manufactures.' Then Burke lamented: 'The age of chivalry is gone; that of sophisters, economists, and calculators has succeeded, and the glory of Europe is extinguished forever.' It was noble rhetoric, and many responded with assent, but others sought to argue by means of a small pamphlet war. The *Reflections* sold over thirty thousand copies, but the most famous answer, Thomas Paine's *The Rights of Man*, circulated in cheap editions, sold several hundred thousand. Paine's work ridiculed the often inflated language of Burke and accused Burke of pitying the plumage but forgetting the dying bird. Paine denied the right of one generation to bind another to a form of government and asserted that the constitution should be the act of the people and justified the French Revolution.

The heat with which much of this public discussion was conducted resulted soon in a suspicion of all reform, and even the mild reforms that had been introduced and voted upon in parliament during the preceding decade were held to be tainted with Jacobinism. Burke's warning that the course of Revolution would only lead to greater bloodshed, war, and an ultimate military despotism proved, as events turned out, to be an accurate prophecy. The initial response to his essay and the pamphlet warfare led to fear on the part of the public and the Home Office, as violence and anarchy seemed to be ascendant over not only France but much of Europe. The Habeas Corpus Act was repealed, governmental spying was common, and prosecution, imprisonment, and transportation awaited those found guilty of inciting the people to revolt by their writing, lecturing, or public discussion.

In France, meanwhile, everything had moved from one extreme to the other. The King, after being forced to accept a constitution, was ultimately deprived of all power, imprisoned, and, finally, on January 21, 1793, executed. The Parisian mob assumed control of the government, and any hope of social, religious, or political freedom in France was over by the middle of 1792. The first military ventures of the new French government were unsuccessful, but new leaders came forth, and France soon was winning all her battles. Her final success in winning the Netherlands led to a break with Britain, and Pitt, who sought for peaceful solutions to the end, had finally to accept what was inevitable. France in February, 1793, one month after the execution of the King, declared war on England.

England had been at war with France many times during the preceding century, but this war was – or seemed to be – different because the French had proclaimed themselves as opposed to all old tyrannies and hereditary monarchies. The issues were not quite so simple as those for the old dynastic struggles of the seventeenth and eighteenth centuries. For this struggle seemed to be a struggle for the minds and hearts of men. However violent and revolting the excesses of the revolutionists were at the moment, these were felt to be a prelude to a better day. Those who held some such faith thought of themselves as citizens of the world rather than of one particular country, for brotherhood knew no national boundaries, nor did the slogan of the Revolution of liberty, fraternity, and equality.

But the declaration of war between the two countries altered the situation of all sympathizers with the Revolution, for now they could be suspected and prosecuted for treason should their activities be too public, too enthusiastic, or too indiscreet. Writing and publication of material held to be seditious was especially likely to receive attention from the authorities. By 1794 prosecutions were frequent. Several printers and booksellers were convicted and imprisoned because of printing and distributing pamphlets held to be seditious. Nice discriminations into degree of affiliation with the enemy or the degree of danger involved were neither sought nor desired. How great was the danger to individuals is not a question easily answered. As long as the books, pamphlets, and discussion were read and discussed in the parlor, government seems not to have worried. Pitt's well-known remark about not being disturbed about Godwin's *Enquiry* (1793) because of its price of three guineas is an apt reminder. But Paine's works were widely read at ale-houses and other resorts of working men, and revolution, although it never came to England, was still feared by those who had not the advantage of being able to read later history. But mob outbreaks had been frequent and serious. In 1780 the Gordon riots in London showed that violence was possible on a large and fearsome scale, and the simultaneous riots in Bath and Bristol, where houses were burned, also showed that it could spread quickly to other parts of the kingdom. In those days before the introduction of police, the constables were really unable to contain any major outbreak, and London was to experience a great many serious disturbances. What part the reading of pamphlets and articles of a seditious nature may have had in arousing the populace to these violent acts is not easily ascertainable, but to prosecute author, printer, and publisher at least gave the authorities the feeling that they were doing something to deal with the issue. In London, the London Corresponding Society felt the heavy hand of public authority. Its secretary, Thomas Hardy, a shoemaker; John Thelwall, a lecturer; John Horne Tooke, a philologist and former associate of John Wilkes – all were accused of treason, and in a celebrated trial, whose defence was conducted by the eloquent Thomas Erskine, were acquitted of the charges. In Scotland, however, prosecution under the irascible septuagenarian judge, Lord Braxfield, resulted in the sentencing of Thomas Palmer, Thomas Muir, and Joseph Gerrald to transportation for treasonable publications and for sponsoring a meeting protesting the war. The failure of the prosecution in London led to an end or lessening of the danger to individuals, but the severity of the punishment in Scotland called forth indignation. Palmer and Muir were 'gentlemen'; Palmer was a graduate of Eton and Cambridge, and Muir was from a landed family. Southey refers to all of them in his poems and in his letters; to him and his friends they were martyrs. Some of those who were prosecuted may not always have been discreet, and their statements and activities may often be said to have provoked the action against them, but their sufferings seem today out of all proportion to their offences. For Muir, Palmer, and Gerrald, it meant the end of any useful life or career; for Hardy, Tooke, and Thelwall, the end of any career in the public eye. With these examples any young writer or speaker would know that some caution would be the better part of wisdom.

THE LITERARY SCENE

The literary scene during the last decade of the eighteenth century was notable for the absence of any single dominating author or groups of authors. The leading poet, William Cowper (1731–1800), whose *Task* (1785) and translations of the *Iliad* and *Odyssey* were widely read, was inactive and living in retirement. The great literary figures of the eighteenth century – Johnson, Gray, Fielding, Smollett, Goldsmith, Sterne – were all dead, and Boswell's celebrated biography of Johnson in 1791 was a reminder of past glories. Within this decade the work of Cowper and the Scottish poet Robert Burns stand out. But other voices were heard. The Gothic novel flourished under the pen of Mrs Anne Radcliffe, whose tales of adventures, often set in Italy in mysterious castles, involving seemingly supernatural events, and introducing scenes of wild and sublime landscape with hero-villains, and beautiful and highly accomplished young ladies in distress, were popular and provided the models for countless novels in the genre. M. G. Lewis's *The Monk* (1797) was a *succès de scandale* with supernatural horrors and criminal deeds. Another type of novel to flourish during this decade was the novel of revolutionary ideas, most notably Godwin's *Caleb Williams* (1794), Robert Bage's *Hermsprong* (1796), Thomas Holcroft's *Anna St. Ives* (1792). In poetry the tame sonnets of William Lisle Bowles (1789) with their quiet descriptions of nature found willing readers in Southey and Coleridge, who in their enthusiasm copied out their favorites to share with their friends and whose own sonnets descriptive of nature in her quieter moods are palpable imitations. More importantly perhaps than imaginative literature during this period were controversial works discussing the new ideas. William Godwin's *Enquiry* and Burke's *Reflections on the Revolution in France* stand out. In areas outside political and ideological controversy appeared many works of travel – Arthur Young's *Travels in France* (1792), Captain William Bligh's account (in 1790) of the mutiny on the *Bounty*, William Gilpin's various travels in search of the picturesque, and, most notable of all, James Boswell's *Life of Johnson* (1791). In poetry and fiction the great names were to appear. During the 1790s the poems of William Blake (*Songs of Innocence* and *Songs of Experience*) were issued almost unnoticed, and in 1798 so were *Lyrical Ballads*. The first twenty years of the nineteenth century, however, were to witness a succession of popular poems from many writers, notably Scott and Byron; an amazing number of novels from Scott and Austen; and a truly astounding number of able essays in prose from Lamb, Hazlitt, De Quincey. The truth seems to be that Southey – with a large number of his contemporaries eager for literary fame – and whatever fortune might come with that fame – came upon the literary scene when the reading public was eager for new names, new themes, and new styles of writing.

During the eighteenth century authorship had become a means whereby a few writers were able to earn a living by their pens, and a very few to achieve a small fortune. Literacy was growing and continued to grow. There was a considerable market for books, and acquaintance with new books and new authors became something of a mark of social and cultural obligation and standing. Letters and memoirs of the eighteenth and early nineteenth centuries are filled with references to reading the latest works of the press. Magazines had a large circulation. The *Gentleman's Magazine* still held its own, and newer miscellanies such as the *Monthly Magazine* (1796) elicited the support of the liberal dissenters and afforded an audience for early works of Southey, Coleridge, and Lamb. The *Edinburgh Review* (1802) and the *Quarterly Review* (1809) were to revolutionize reviewing and periodical authorship. Articles on politics (the mainstay of both reviews) were supplemented by substantial, authoritative articles on history, science, classical literature and antiquities, as well as slighter articles on poetry, fiction, and essays. The high quality – and the high pay of ten guineas per sheet for the contributors – determined and assured the success of both quarterlies. Other periodicals emulated the example of these two publications and hoped for a similar success. *Blackwood's Edinburgh Magazine*, although Tory in politics, welcomed fiction and poetry after its founding in 1817. The *London Magazine* (1820) published a number of 'classics': Lamb's masterpiece, his essays of Elia, parts of De Quincey's *Confessions of an English Opium Eater*, Hazlitt's *Table Talk* with occasional bits from Keats, Clare, and Hood. The periodicals provided not only an important pecuniary support for authors but also fostered a discussion of political, social, and controversial intellectual issues among the literate and educated classes. A sentence should also be given to the newspapers, for they too provided some outlet for writers and modest remuneration, notably the *Morning Chronicle* for which Coleridge and Hazlitt contributed, and the *Morning Post* for Coleridge and Southey who was for 1798 and 1799 Daniel Stuart's laureate at a guinea a week. Southey was to complain for most of his life that he was never able to give up reviewing – it should be pointed out that many reviews were in essence not so much reviews as essays inspired by the material of the book under review. Reviewing served to broaden his interests and to make him think and learn about a variety of subjects – historical, geographical, and social – which a narrow regimen devoted solely to belles-lettres would not have done.

But books were the avenue by which a writer could make a fortune. None of the poets such as Southey, Coleridge, Wordsworth of their generation or Keats and Shelley of the next generation ever made more than modest sums from any of their books, poetry or prose, but Scott and Byron earned huge sums from their works. Byron demanded £2,625 for the fourth canto of *Childe Harold*, and Scott's earnings were legendary. Popularity brought not only wealth but fame and recognition. Scott and Byron became household names. And even writers who did not begin to share such popularity amid all classes or readers received their share of recognition. Southey, who did not enjoy the widest popularity, found himself the object of much interest: in 1813, the year of his appointment as laureate, his letters describe numerous parties and celebrities, and he even used the name of lion to describe his situation. Later in life (1835) Peel offered him a baronetcy, which he declined, but Scott's baronetcy is well known, and a later poet, Tennyson, was granted a peerage. Authorship thus could be the avenue for not only a respectable livelihood, but if the fates smiled, a fortune and a title.

Oxford, Pantisocracy, Coleridge, and Poetry

Southey's entrance at Oxford in mid-January, 1793 was not one of joyous anticipation. His rejection at Christ Church, where most of his Westminster friends were enrolled, may have had something to do with his feeling. 'My prepossessions are not very favourable; I expect to meet with pedantry, prejudice, and aristocracy, from all which good Lord deliver poor Robert Southey,' he wrote Bedford (*Life*, vol. 1, p. 169). Later he said that all he learned at Oxford was how to row and swim (*Life*, vol. 1, p. 176n), but this statement is an exaggeration, and despite the gloomy anticipation of what he would find at Balliol, he found many compensations, such as leisure for reading, writing, and the inevitable sociability where groups of young men are resident. Although he had no ready-made friends from Westminster at Balliol, he soon made new ones, of which the most influential was Edmund Seward. Three years older than Southey, Seward (1771–95) – from what we can infer from Southey's references to him – was a young man of remarkable self-control, of ascetic habits, and of considerable academic attainments achieved by regular, unremitting study. 'Two years ago Seward drank wine, eat butter and sugar, now merely from the resolution of abridging the luxuries of life water is his only drink, tea and dry toast his only breakfast' (*New Letters*, vol. 1, p. 16). Years later Southey wrote: 'I loved him with my whole heart, and shall remember him with gratitude and affection as one who was my moral father, to the last moment of my life' (*Life*, vol. 4, p. 320). The poem 'The Dead Friend' is Southey's poetic commemoration of this friendship. Another friend from Balliol days was Richard Duppa, artist and author. Southey found aspects of Balliol and Oxford not at all to his liking. There were the pompous and bewigged fellows for whom he felt little respect although his own tutor, Thomas Howe, seems to have been easy-going, amiable, and undemanding. He told Southey at the outset that he had little or nothing to teach him. Southey complained of one imposed exercise on the January 30, anniversary of the beheading of Charles I, which somewhat offended his anti-monarchial sentiments, but he found it easier to comply with the assignment than to speak overmuch of Milton (*New Letters*, vol. 1, p. 164). Not only did Southey object to the general air of stuffiness among the authorities – a recurrent complaint of undergraduates of all generations – but of intemperance and vice among many of the students. He believed, in fact, that some of the old discipline of monastic days could be employed to advantage as restrictions upon the behavior of the students. 'Temperance is much wanted; the waters of Helicon are far too much polluted by the wine of Bacchus ever to produce any effect' was his comment on the students with the additional general phrase of 'every species of abandoned excess.' For the 'superior, Oxford only exhibits waste of wigs and want of wisdom.'

But Southey did not let his disapproval of some aspects of life at Balliol interfere with his own pursuits. He kept up his friendships with such Old Westminsters as Wynn of Christ Church in boating on the Isis and walking expeditions in the country. During the Easter vacation of 1793 there was a long trip with Seward to visit his family in Herefordshire. Days were filled with reading and the writing of poems, the first version of *Joan of Arc* in particular. Vacations were spent on a round of visits, chiefly to the Bedfords at Brixton. His mother, since the bankruptcy and death of Southey's father in 1792, was keeping a lodging house in Bath. It was not a profitable or congenial enterprise, and life for Mrs Southey was made more difficult by the bullying of her sister.

Much of Southey's uneasiness at Oxford was certainly due to worries over money. On December 11, 1793 he described his situation to Horace Bedford in some detail:

> You know my father was a tradesman, in those circumstances
> which enabled him for twenty years to live happily and support
> a family in that honourable mediocrity most to be envied. Three
> years back he became the dupe of artifice and was ruined. He
> struggled in vain with misfortunes. An unfeeling brother refused
> assistance, and he was arrested not for his own debts but for a
> bill indorsed for a deceitful friend. I saw him Horace in prison.
> I saw him released just in time to reach home – meet fresh
> misfortunes and die of a broken heart (*New Letters*, vol. 1, p. 36).

His support came from his uncle Herbert Hill, and since his conscientious scruples made it increasingly difficult to take holy orders, subscribe to the Thirty-nine Articles, and be a country clergyman, he worried over how much longer he could accept this support. Mr Hill, as Southey's letters to John May make clear, contributed substantially to the financial support of his sisters Miss Tyler and Mrs Southey and the four Southey children. His own income was derived from estates

in Herefordshire and his salary as the chaplain to the British Factory
in Lisbon. Because of his residence in Lisbon his business at home was
tended to by an agent, William Bowyer Thomas of Hereford. There
were occasions during 1793 and 1794 when Southey seems literally to
have had no money and would have gone without a meal unless a
friend had provided him with one. Much can be understood about
Southey if the struggle of the early years can be remembered. Although
of short duration, the precariousness of his situation in life was early
brought home to him. A dominant theme in his letters and in his
occasional poetry is the desire for a settled home, peace, and security.
These things he never had in childhood or young manhood. Shunted
from his parents' home in Bristol to Miss Tyler's various eccentric
establishments, and to a series of schools – Corston, Westminster, and
Oxford – he never had for any length of time a settled domicile.
Indeed, until he moved to Greta Hall at Keswick in 1803 he lived as
both single and married man in a succession of temporary lodgings.

Southey stated that he learned nothing at Oxford except rowing
and swimming, and since his letters do not mention his studies but
rather social meetings with friends, excursions in the country, reading,
and the writing of verse, that statement may well be true. His concern
over his future and his unwillingness to take holy orders led him to
cast about for alternative careers. In the winter of 1794 he thought of
medicine:

> I purpose studying physic: innumerable and insuperable
> objections appeared to divinity . . . a liberal education precludes
> the man of no fortune from independence in the humbler lines
> of life; he may either turn soldier or embrace one of three
> professions, in all of which there is too much quackery. . . . Very
> soon I shall commence my anatomical and chemical studies (*Life*,
> vol. 1, p. 204).

But medical study proved uncongenial. As Cuthbert Southey phrased
it: '. . . he soon abandoned the idea as hastily as he had adopted it;
partly from being unable to overcome his disgust to a dissecting-room,
and partly because the love of literary pursuits was so strong within
him.' One result, however, of this brief exposure to medicine was a
life-long interest in the subject, evidenced in many extracts from
medical writers in *The Doctor*, an interest later enhanced by the medical
studies and career of his brother Henry Herbert.

The date of Southey's engagement to Edith Fricker cannot be

precisely determined. In his lengthy letters to his friends he talks about every subject under the sun, but he is silent about his feelings towards Edith. The Fricker family consisted of a mother – the deceased father is described as having been a manufacturer of sugar pans – five daughters (Sarah, Edith, Mary, Martha, and Eliza) and one son George. Southey had known the Frickers since childhood. The Frickers were obviously in modest financial circumstances, but whether the sisters were ever 'milliners of Bath' – to use Byron's picturesque phrase – cannot be established. They may well have needed to earn money, and some employment in the line of dressmaking or hatmaking may have come to them. The two youngest sisters, Martha and Eliza, were later referred to as 'mantua-makers.' All these speculations as to the possible employment of the Fricker sisters aside, the fact appears that by June, 1794 Southey was thinking of marriage, and the letters for the rest of the year show that he was very much a part of the Fricker family circle.

Southey's letter of June 1, 1794 to Grosvenor Bedford reveals his state of mind and his real confusion concerning his future. He was now convinced that he could not take orders, and sought some situation in London. Having come to this decision, there was no point in continuing at Oxford since his uncle had placed him there in the hope that he would ultimately enter the church. 'The official situation is more an object of temporary convenience than future necessity. I want an obvious reason for abandoning Oxford and a certainty of existence till my own ability allow me to marry.' In the event that the situation in London was not forthcoming there was always emigration. Whatever occurred, Southey had confidence in his own abilities. 'Were I once settled in London I have not the smallest doubt of success' (*New Letters*, vol. 1, p. 54).

In this uncertain situation Southey's whole future was changed by what seemed to be a chance meeting. The meeting was with Coleridge, whom he met through Robert Allen (1772–1805), whom he in turn had met during his course of attending the medical lectures, and who was an old friend of Coleridge's from Christ's Hospital School. The friendship between the two was instantaneous. 'Allen is with us daily and his friend from Cambridge, Coleridge,' he wrote Bedford, '. . . He is of most uncommon merit – of the strongest genius, the clearest judgment, the best heart. My friend he already is and must hereafter be yours' (*New Letters*, vol. 1, p. 58). This letter of the middle of June shows a great lift of spirits. The first result was a scheme to establish a kind of ideal society, a 'pantisocracy,' built upon Southey's earlier idea of emigrating to America. Such a scheme would settle Southey's most pressing problems: it would give him an occupation, and it would enable him to marry. It is not possible to assign details of the scheme to one or other of the protagonists, but it is evident that there were long and animated sessions of talk, and the details emerged. Some of the nomenclature sounds rather like Coleridge – pantisocracy itself – a Greek word meaning the equal rule of all – and another Greek word, aspheterism, meaning that property would be held in common. 'These, Tom, are two new words, the first signifying the equal government of all, and the other the generalization of individual property' (*Life*, vol. 1, p. 221). The most complete description of pantisocracy comes from the pen of Thomas Poole, whom Coleridge and Southey visited later in the summer.

Twelve gentlemen of good education and liberal principles are to embark with twelve ladies in April next. Previous to their leaving this country they are to have as much intercourse as possible, in order to ascertain each other's dispositions, and firmly to settle every regulation for the government of their future conduct. Their opinion was that they should fix themselves at – I do not recollect the place, but somewhere in a delightful part of the new back settlements; that each man should labour two or three hours in a day, the produce of which labour would, they imagine, be more than sufficient to support the colony. As Adam Smith observes that there is not above one productive man in twenty, they argue that if each laboured the twentieth part of time, it would produce enough to satisfy their wants. The produce of their industry is to be laid up in common for the use of all; and a good library of books is to be collected, and their leisure hours to be spent in study, liberal discussions, and the education of their children. A system for the education of their children is laid down, for which, if this plan at all suits you, I must refer you to the authors of it. The regulations relating to the females strike them as the most difficult; whether the marriage contract shall be dissolved if agreeable to one or both parties, and many other circumstances, are not yet determined. The employments of the women are to be the care of infant children, and other occupations suited to their strength; at the same time the greatest attention is to be paid to the cultivation of their minds. Every one is to enjoy his own religious and political opinions, provided they do not encroach on the rules previously made, which rules, it is unnecessary to add, must in some measure be regulated by the laws of the state which includes the district in which they settle. They calculate that each gentleman providing £125 will be sufficient to carry the scheme into execution. Finally, every individual is at liberty, whenever he pleases, to withdraw from the society (Mrs Henry Sandford, *Thomas Poole and His Friends*, London, 1888, I, p. 98).

Whether all these details were agreed upon during the brief visit of Coleridge at Oxford is debatable; they probably belong to the late summer when both instigators of the scheme were in Bristol. From Oxford Coleridge proceeded according to his plan on a walking tour of Wales with Joseph Hucks, while Southey withdrew from Oxford in July, never to return. For the next year Southey lived at various places in Bath and Bristol, with his mother, with Miss Tyler, and shared rooms in Bristol with Coleridge.

The summer and fall of 1794 were busy and lively times. Coleridge and Southey acted upon each other in stimulating ways. Coleridge's conversational powers and personal charm won over Southey completely. It is not hard to see that Coleridge was the sharpest mind and the most widely read of all the young men Southey had ever met. Moreover, he shared the hopes and aspirations for better days and all the revolutionary enthusiasms and points of view which were in the air. Southey's two best friends, Wynn and Bedford, did not share such hopes and were frankly sceptical of the brave new world that seemed to be dawning. Southey argued with Bedford who declaimed 'against Levellers and Jacobines' (*New Letters*, vol. 1, p. 67), but Bedford seemed quite happy to live undisturbed in the modest government position in which he was to spend his life. Wynn's prospects, of course, were assured, and his aristocratic Whig family could see that his abilities had ample scope for employment and recognition.

Southey did not spend all the summer and autumn in the promotion of pantisocracy, but rather in writing and reading. *Joan of Arc* he had finished at Oxford, and he hoped to revise it for publication. Many of his short poems he had selected and was to publish in a joint volume with Robert Lovell, a young man of Quaker family who had recently married Mary Fricker. He was also hoping (in vain) the publisher Johnson would publish his 'Botany Bay Eclogues.' By September 7 he and Coleridge had written within twenty-four hours a joint play, *The Fall of Robespierre*. This hastily written production – some of it versified accounts of the newspaper reports of the convention which decreed the end of Robespierre – was published under Coleridge's name, but the second and third acts were of Southey's composition. A short work of under eight hundred lines of blank verse, the play contained many a glance at Julius Caesar and Brutus. These few lines may serve as a sample of the rhetoric:

> Was it for this we hurl'd proud Capet down?
> Is it for this we wage eternal war
> Against the tyrant horde of murderers,
> The crowned cockatrices whose foul venom
> Infects all Europe?
>
> (II, 263–7)

By October 12 his *Poems*, published by Cruttwell of Bath, was printed. This joint volume of *Poems* with Lovell used the pseudonym Bion for Southey's poems and Moschus for Lovell's. The poems were derivative from late eighteenth-century models of William Lisle Bowles, the Wartons, Collins, and Gray – one of Lovell's being a frank imitation of the celebrated 'Elegy.' Southey's later judgment was wise, saving only 'The Retrospect' for later reprinting and letting the others rest in the decent obscurity of what is today a rare little volume.

By his twentieth birthday – August 12 – Southey was firm in his resolution to quit England for America. Pantisocracy was the dominant interest, March of 1795 having been set as the date for emigration. 'It is my duty to depart,' he informed Horace Bedford. 'At present everything smiles upon the undertaking. Should the resolution of others fail, Coleridge and I will go together. . . . We go at least twelve men with women and children; my Mother accompanies me, who will then not be the only Mrs Southey. The woman whom I love has consented to go with her sisters. Burnett Allen Coleridge Lovell etc. . . . We purchase a thousand acres, hire labourers to assist us in clearing it and building houses. By this day twelvemonths the Pantiso-cratic society of Aspheterists will be settled on the banks of the Susque-hannah' (*New Letters*, vol. 1, pp. 70–1). Before concluding the same letter Southey went on: 'My mind is never at rest not even for a moment. One grand object has fully possessed my soul.' And all this when two months before he had been an anxious student at Oxford wondering where next he might turn! Pantisocracy, his new friendship with Coleridge, and the prospect of marriage had completely transformed his life.

There was still time to be stirred by the news from the Continent. There can be no doubt that both Southey and Coleridge were completely in sympathy with the radical and Jacobin position. The following paragraph from Southey's letter to his brother Tom on October 12 shows his devotion to all the ideals to which the Revolution had been committed and to his unwillingness to let the violence, bloodshed, and war in which the French were engaged alter his faith:

> The allies are every where defeated, the French every where
> victorious – the cause of Liberty every where gaining ground.
> The Poles are successful and the tyrant of Prussia totters upon his
> blood-cemented throne. Holland is on the point of ruin. In Spain
> nothing can oppose the Sans Culottes. Germany is beggared – the
> blood and treasures of England lavished by a corrupt adminis-
> tration. The sword of iniquity is drawn. Two men suffer next
> week at Edinburgh for high treason. It is apprehended that
> Thelwall, Horn Tooke, and Thomas Holcroft etc. will share the
> same fate. The measure of iniquity must soon be full and then –
> (*New Letters*, vol. 1, p. 81).

Another burst of literary activity resulting from the stimulation of the new-found friendship with Coleridge was the writing in three days of the play *Wat Tyler*, a work that would have been forgotten except for its piratical publication in 1817, twenty-three years later. The history of the attempt to publish seems to be that Lovell late in the year 1794 took the manuscript to Ridgeway, a publisher, and sought to have it published. Southey visited Ridgeway in January, 1795, in Newgate, the only time he was ever in that prison, about its publication. Although Ridgeway and Symmonds, also a prisoner, agreed to print the play, and share the profits, the work was not printed.

The play, written so hastily, is not without verve and liveliness. The characters are portrayed in black and white. Wat Tyler is hard-working, domestically oriented towards wife and daughter, and beset by poverty and high taxes, which the king and courtiers are wasting upon their own luxurious living and the pursuit of a war with France. Wat Tyler and John Ball, the priest, are opposed to the war in which they feel no interest and are strongly opposed to all forms of tyranny in both church and state. In the violence Tyler is killed and Ball, as the play ends, calmly awaits execution, firm in the knowledge that he has suffered in a good cause. 'For I am armed with rectitude of soul,' he states and is confident that

> The destined hour must come
> When it shall blaze with sun-surpassing splendor,
> And the dark mists of prejudice and falsehood
> Fade in its strong effulgence.

The autumn months of 1794 were heady and stimulating. During these months and those of early 1795, Southey and Coleridge shared rooms on College Street in a lodging house run by Mrs Savier. They were as close as two friends could be, talking together, reading, planning works of great magnitude, encouraging and advising each other. Indeed, many of the works of Coleridge and Southey were collaborations such as *The Fall of Robespierre* and a long passage in *Joan of Arc* (later excerpted by Coleridge as 'The Destiny of Nations'). Books were read – they had access to the Bristol Library – and short trips and excursions were made, of which the visit to Thomas Poole was one. But it was inevitable that at some time the intimacy between the two would break since differences that could lead to quarrels were inevitable. Much of the attraction between Coleridge and Southey was that of opposites, and it was the opposite quality of each that led to friction. The fascination of Coleridge's conversation and his infectious enthusiasms came to Southey at a time when he was uncertain over his future prospects. The new friend and the new-found scheme of pantisocracy gave him a new life and new hope, and for the first time he met someone whose genius could really stimulate him and whose enthusiasm for the new revolutionary ideas he could share as he could not with old Westminster friends and such Balliol friends as Edmund Seward. The stability and earnestness of Southey's temperament appealed to Coleridge, but Southey soon found that in the joint establishment he was the one who often performed the duties and met the deadlines, and he came to feel that he was bearing more than his share of the burden. Since both were about as impecunious as anyone can be, these were important considerations. Southey, two years younger than Coleridge, had obligations to others which he felt he could not ignore.

In addition to their writing, both Southey and Coleridge lectured in Bristol. Southey's historical lectures – the prospectus is in *Life*, I, 234–5 – were twelve in number and the tickets for the whole course were 12s. 6d. The lectures were nothing if not ambitious; covering history from the 'Origin and Progress of Society' and concluding with the American War. One lecture in the midst of the series was devoted to the Eastern Empire and the rise of Mahomet. The lectures do not survive, but there is some account of them. Southey worked hard at his lectures in order to have enough information for two lectures a week of an hour's length. He spoke disparagingly of them as only 'splendid declamation' but they were attended 'by all who love good Republicans and odd characters' (*New Letters*, vol. 1, pp. 92–3). An anonymous admirer of Southey wrote an account of the lectures in *The Observer, Part I being a Transient Glance at About Forty Youths of Bristol*, published during the summer or fall of 1795:

> He has lately delivered some Lectures in this City, which ought to draw from all men their most warm approbation; the language was that of Truth; it was the language of Liberty. I must here observe that his gesticulation and attitude when he is speaking in Public is not the most pleasing, his body is always too stiff, his features are apt to be distorted; they are faults which he can easily obviate; if he do, I am bold to say, that he will possess Demosthenian or Ciceronian abilities. From what has been adduced it is almost unnecessary to say, that he is really the man of virtue according to the present state of society (quoted in *New Letters*, vol. 1, p. 42n).

Southey commented further at the end of the lectures that he had 'said bolder truths than any other Man in this country yet ventured. Speaking of my friend Tom I cried O Paine! hireless Priest of Liberty! unbought teacher of the poor!' (*New Letters*, vol. 1, p. 94). Southey does not appear ever again to have graced the lecture platform. Although friends and acquaintances were later to testify to the charm and ease of his conversation, he seems to have found public speaking uncongenial to his talents.

Southey's appearance as a young man was attractive. Joseph Cottle, who met Southey through Robert Lovell during the last months of 1794, recalled his first meeting:

> Never will the impression be effaced, produced on me by this young man. Tall, dignified, possessing great suavity of manners; an eye piercing, with a countenance full of genius, kindliness, and intelligence.

Cottle also attended the lectures and spoke of Southey's self-possession before this 'polite and discriminating audience' (*Reminiscences*, p. 26). Early portraits by Hancock and Sharples confirm this impressionistic description by Cottle. They reveal an aquiline nose, a full head of dark hair, and a self-confident air. Throughout his life Southey remained lean – he compared himself to a greyhound, and his height of five feet and eleven inches made him considerably taller than the average man of his day.

The lectures, however, were to bring a disagreement between Coleridge and Southey since, according to Cottle, Coleridge agreed to deliver one of Southey's lectures, then having agreed, failed to appear. This failure of Coleridge to live up to his promise led to a dispute and recrimination. Other disappointments contributed to strained relations. The original plan of the pantisocrats had been to sail in March, but March found them in Bristol lecturing to 'polite and discriminating' audiences, to repeat Cottle's phrase. Various persons who had originally been persuaded withdrew, among them Southey's mother. Everyone lacked the one thing needful – money – since it would take a considerable sum to pay the passage, to buy land, and to provide for subsistence until the property should become self-supporting. A suggestion that pantisocracy be tried in Wales came to nothing.

Southey's departure from Oxford during July and resumption of his Bristol-Bath residence were not to prove peaceful. As he awaited Coleridge's arrival in Bristol so that plans for the pantisocratic settlement could be advanced, he had much to do by way of getting works ready for the press. *Joan of Arc*, which he had completed at Oxford, was in need not only of revision but of a publisher or of subscribers. There were also short poems, sonnets and odes, to be published. For this second venture a collaborator appeared in Robert Lovell, who did Southey the further good service of introducing him to the young bookseller, Joseph Cottle. Whatever can be said of Cottle's vanity and his overestimation of his own literary powers, he had what Southey always credited him with – a good and generous heart. He came forward with an offer to publish *Joan of Arc*; he later published several of Southey's works and the celebrated *Lyrical Ballads* in 1798.

But in mid-October a melodramatic domestic crisis arose. Miss Tyler discovered the plan for a pantisocracy. Her anger and rage knew no bounds. Although it was a rainy, stormy night she literally expelled her nephew from the house, and he walked all the way to Bath that night. "'Amid the pelting of the pitiless storm' did I, Robert Southey, the Apostle of Pantisocracy, depart from the city of Bristol, my natal place – at the hour of five in a wet windy evening on the 17th of October, 1794, wrapped up in my father's old great coat, and my own cogitations. . . . I reached not Bath till nine o'clock. "I will never see his face again [writes Miss Tyler]"' (*Letters of S. T. Coleridge*, ed. E. H. Coleridge, Boston, 1895, I, 107n–8n).

The year 1795 brought decisive changes in Southey's life. After the lectures of the spring and the attempts to earn money from writing, the basic problem of his settlement in life remained unsolved. As the year advanced the dream of the wonderful new life in America faded, but other events were to occur that would change his life and determine his career. The Reverend Mr Hill, wise and understanding, accepted the fact that his nephew was not going to take holy orders and return to Oxford, and generously suggested that he pay a lengthy visit to Lisbon. Charles Wynn during the year recommended that Southey undertake the study of law, and to underscore his faith in the ability of Southey to make a name for himself, either in literature or law, or in some happy combination of the two, offered to grant him an annuity of £160 per year on his own coming of age in 1796. In the meantime the fall and winter in Lisbon would give Southey the chance to assess his situation and relieve him of the pressure of the struggle for a day-to-day existence. But always in the background of the decisions which others were making for his future was his determination to marry Edith Fricker, to whom he had become engaged in 1794. He said very little about the matter in his correspondence with others, but his action was decisive, for on the eve of his departure for Portugal with his uncle he married Edith Fricker at the historic church of St Mary Redcliffe on November 14, 1795. Later he told Cottle of his appreciation for the latter's part in the arrangements: Cottle gave him the money for the ring, and Edith found a home with Cottle's sister Mary.

But while these events were taking place, Coleridge and Southey had been drifting apart. Coleridge might well feel that he was left out of any share in Southey's arrangements, and that Southey was going ahead selfishly thinking only of his own future to the neglect of his friend with whom he had shared the closest thoughts and who had collaborated in what were to be such mighty works. It all culminated in a letter of recrimination on November 13, 1795 in which Coleridge reviewed his association with Southey and poured out all his resentments and frustrations in a long series of accusations – ten pages of print in the *Collected Letters*. This letter made a future reconciliation difficult, and one did not happen until 1797.

2

1796-1843

Portugal, Spain, London, Law, and Literature

Portugal was a new experience and a new chapter in Southey's life.
There were many things to be gained from this residence and travel.
For one thing he came under the guidance of his uncle, a tactful and
understanding man, of considerable educational attainments, learned
in the history and literature of his adopted country of Portugal, a
collector of books and manuscripts, and the mainstay of the Southey
family. He moved, as far as we can tell, in somewhat higher circles
than Southey. As the British chaplain in Lisbon he knew the British
diplomats and some from other countries. Mr Hill was a stable personality, somewhat versed in the manners and ways of the world,
and a scholar, who could direct Southey's readings in Portuguese
history. Although Mr Hill had made important decisions about
Southey's education at school and college, the two were virtual
strangers to each other having met only at long intervals during Mr
Hill's infrequent visits to England. Mr Hill was to fulfil the role of an
older man to whom Southey could look for guidance and with respect
and affection. During his boyhood and schooling at Westminster and
Oxford he had never met anyone who filled that influential role.

The first trip to Portugal and Spain can be minutely traced by the
travel book which Southey compiled on his return to England. *Letters
Written During a Short Residence in Spain and Portugal* is a work hastily
put together from notes and heavily padded by translations and peri-
pheral materials. It describes the arduous land journey from Coruña,
the port of landing, to Madrid, and thence to Lisbon, and provides a
detailed account of the places visited and the discomforts of travelling.
The journey by stage coach, the stops at inns, where the beds often
had to be shared with fleas and the food was scarcely edible by English

tastes, was one of considerable discomfort during the cold days of December and January. Southey appears to have been – perhaps from the early training from Miss Tyler – rather more sensitive to dirt and filth than the average person, and he was shocked by the omnipresence of dirt – the very streets seem to have been used as much for sewers and the disposal of trash as for transportation. Byron's impression of Lisbon many years later was the same:

> For hut and palace show like filthily:
> The dingy denizens are rear'd in dirt;
> Ne personage of high or mean degree
> Doth care for cleanness of surtout or shirt.

> (*Childe Harold*, I, 229–32)

However far from twentieth-century standards of hygiene and cleanliness eighteenth-century England may have been, it is obvious that the English were accustomed to a far higher standard of sanitation and creature comforts than were the Spaniards and Portuguese. All travellers – especially those on their first trip from home – are fascinated by the picturesqueness and the differences of architecture, scenery, and the physical appearance and dress of the inhabitants, but at the same time they are discomfited by those differences that deprive them of their usual diet and physical comforts. The knowledge, however, which Southey gained by this long journey through Spain was of advantage to him when he came to write the history of the Peninsular War because many of the military manoeuvres were along the very roads he travelled, and also for his long poem *Roderick*, set in medieval Spain. First-hand familiarity with the Spanish scene was to be of inestimable value.

At Lisbon Southey settled down into a routine of writing, study, and social activity, which Mr Hill's position procured for him. His first feeling on finally reaching Lisbon after thirty-three days on the road was to count the days until his return to England, but the routine of study and writing and the warmth and beauty of the winter and spring in Lisbon soon altered this feeling.

By February, 1796 Southey spoke with facility in both Spanish and Portuguese, and one of his tasks was the translation of poems from Spanish and Portuguese, some of which are scattered throughout his *Letters Written During a Short Residence in Spain and Portugal*. More serious study was in the history of the peninsula, and here his uncle was his guide. There were many English persons in Portugal either to meet or to hear about. The most conspicuous was the wealthy young William Beckford, author of *Vathek*, about whom there were many scandalous stories, but he was cut by the resident English, and there is no evidence that he and Southey ever met. Many persons in Southey's social circle during the later years of his life were persons whom he met during his two visits to Portugal. Two of his important friendships were the result of his first months in Lisbon: those with John May and Mary Barker. May, a business man of broad cultural interests, a pupil of George Coleridge and friend and patron of John Taylor Coleridge, became a life-long friend and confidant of Southey; Mary Barker, a lively and talented girl in 1796, was later for many years a neighbor in Keswick. Although Southey was not aware of the importance at the time, his few months in Spain and Lisbon were to influence his life significantly. From his residence and from the opportunities for study he received came the impetus to make himself a leading authority upon matters Spanish and Portuguese during his generation and to widen his circle of friends to include those with more cosmopolitan interests than most of those he had previously known. There was, however, one unfortunate aspect to this residence in Spain and Portugal: from it came his determined, life-long, and somewhat unreasoning hatred and distrust of the Roman Catholic Church. He was shocked by what he saw of a Church that appeared to encourage superstition, that was itself filled with corruption, and which only recently had persecuted all dissent with all the terrors of the Inquisition. Its alliance with a venal, incompetent, and corrupt monarchy also contributed to this feeling. England, it is well to remember, was one of the few countries in Europe with religious toleration – the toleration may not have included full rights and privileges for those outside the Established Church, but they were permitted to have their own chapels, and adherents were not imprisoned. Incidentally, Mr Hill was in no sense a missionary to the Portuguese: he was the chaplain to the British factory in Lisbon – that is the association of British factors or merchants resident – and did perform services for British subjects who might be in the country. There was not, however, a church since such a building was at that time not permitted. The present English church – surrounded by a cemetery and enclosed by a high wall – is of later erection.

Southey's return home was in May of 1796. At first he lived with Edith in lodgings at Kingsdown, near Bristol, for the remainder of the year, and was immediately busy with getting his *Letters* ready for the press and pleased with the good reviews of *Joan of Arc*, published during his absence. But concern for the future was still an ever-present anxiety. Wynn's generosity relieved him of some worry, but Wynn expected him to study law, and Southey formally entered Gray's Inn in February, 1797. 'The millstone of dependence hanging round my neck,' as he put it, was irksome (*New Letters*, vol. 1, p. 110). A partial reconciliation with Coleridge took place: Southey wrote him translating a phrase from Schiller: 'Fiesco! Fiesco! thou leavest a void in my bosom, which the human race, thrice told, will never fill up.' But his days were filled with composition. Southey's facility at writing during the years 1796 to 1800 is truly amazing. He was at work getting together a collection of poems that Cottle was to publish at the close of the year – it proved so successful that a second edition was required before the end of 1797 – and he was hard at work at *Madoc* in its first version. He also established an outlet for miscellaneous contributions – from poems to letters on Welsh poetry to accounts and translations of Spanish and Portuguese poetry – in the *Monthly Magazine*, an enterprise of Richard Phillips and the Aikin family, hospitable to new things in literature and politics.

The winter in London was tedious. The study of the law was uncongenial, and Southey certainly spent most of his time in writing, and not in legal study. London gave him the opportunity to see his London friends and to meet such literary and artistic celebrities as Mary Wollstonecraft, William Godwin, and the painter John Opie. London also afforded him the chance to see more of Charles Lamb. Since it was not necessary to keep residence at Gray's Inn during the summer, Southey and Edith went to Burton, a village near Christchurch and near the sea. The surroundings proved congenial and the area was a pleasant one for walks and country excursions. Charles Lloyd, the friend of Lamb, and the unstable member of a prominent Quaker family of bankers from Birmingham, spent part of the summer with the Southeys at Burton. Here it was that Southey presumably helped Lloyd in the composition of his novel, *Edmund Oliver* (1798), with its very thinly disguised portraits of both Southey and Coleridge. For Southey the most important event of the summer of 1797 was the friendship he formed with John Rickman, whom Rickman's biographer Orlo Williams described as 'Lamb's friend the Census Taker.' At this time Rickman at twenty-six had not entered upon any career but was a studious young man whose anti-ministerial views would be congenial to Southey. In appearance and temperament he was rough and reticent in speaking of his feelings but well versed in what today would be called the field of economics. He became secretary to Charles Abbot, Lord Colchester, later the Speaker of the House of Commons; in turn Rickman was to be clerk and secretary of the House and to spend his life in the shadow of Westminster. Charles Lamb visited Southey at Burton. Coleridge was still at a distance, and Lloyd's portrait of Coleridge in his novel and Coleridge's parody of Southey published under the pseudonym of Nehemiah Higginbottom were not designed to foster a complete reconciliation.

September and October were spent in Bath and Bristol, but by December Southey and Edith were back in London. A notable engagement of the years 1798 and 1799 was that of laureate to Daniel Stuart's *Morning Post*, to which Southey regularly contributed poems, both original and translations. Coleridge and Wordsworth also wrote for the *Post* at this time, along with a host of forgotten or nearly forgotten poets and poetesses such as Mrs Mary 'Perdita' Robinson. Some of Southey's most anthologized poems first appeared in the *Morning Post*: 'The Battle of Blenheim,' 'The Well of St. Keyne,' 'The Holly Tree,' and 'God's Judgement on a Wicked Bishop.'

When he was not in London during 1798 and 1799, Southey became Charles Lamb's favorite correspondent, and Lamb became a whole-hearted admirer of Southey's works. During May of 1798 Southey visited Norwich, where his brother Henry Herbert was in school, and there he met William Taylor, the voluminous reviewer for dissenting magazines and one of the earliest students of German literature in England. Taylor became another firm friend of Southey, with whom he corresponded at intervals for a lifetime. Taylor's learning was wide, philological, and often a trifle pedantic, but Taylor's translation of Bürger's 'Lenore' introduced Scott to German balladry. Taylor was one of the pioneers in introducing German literature into England. Reviewing, which was to be a life-long economic necessity for Southey, began in 1797 with reviews for the *Critical Review*. Most of these were brief and hurried, the best remembered and not particularly to Southey's credit was his review of *Lyrical Ballads* in which he called *The Ancient Mariner* 'a Dutch attempt at German sublimity.' His praise was for the more conventional 'Tintern Abbey.'

By early 1799 Southey's health was beginning to pay the price of this unremitting study and writing. The first version of *Madoc* was completed, and *Thalaba* begun. *Joan of Arc* was revised for a second edition which appeared in 1798, and Southey planned an anthology to which he and his friends would contribute short poems. The *Annual*

Anthology appeared for two years, 1799 and 1800, and represents the poetic outpouring of the various poets whom Southey knew and to whom in some ways he served as a center. In addition to the well-known and famous names of Coleridge and Lamb, there was the work of Joseph Cottle, George Dyer, Amelia Opie, William Taylor, Humphry Davy, as well as such literarily obscure friends of his as the Bedford brothers Grosvenor and Horace, James Jennings called 'The Traumatic Poet,' and his late brother-in-law Robert Lovell.

Coleridge and Wordsworth spent the winter of 1798 and 1799 in Germany, and during Coleridge's absence Sara Coleridge had spent part of the time with the Southeys at Westbury near Bristol. The kindness of Southey and his wife after the death of the Coleridges' infant son Berkeley during this absence of the father served further to heal the wounded friendship between Coleridge and Southey. On Coleridge's return in the summer of 1799 Thomas Poole's letter of explanation concerning some of Charles Lloyd's tale-bearing hastened the process of reconciliation. The old intimacy, however, could never be resumed; both young men were five years older and had assumed family responsibilities, and both were absorbed with establishing their careers as authors. The differences in their temperaments were if anything more clearly marked than they had been in 1794, but there was perhaps more tolerance for the differences. The two were now willing to resume their old close association, and most of the late summer – August and September – was spent together in travelling in the west of England and in visits to Ottery St Mary, the seat of the Coleridge family. Letters and Southey's journal (*CPB*, vol. 4, pp. 517–24) give in detail the places and persons visited. Again, the desire for poetical collaboration asserted itself, and the two wrote together 'The Devil's Walk' or 'The Devil's Thoughts' and projected a poem on Mohammed.

Despite the healthful activity of walking and physical exertion of the summer and the stimulation of Coleridge's company, Southey's health did not improve. For the second time an invitation from his uncle to visit Portugal provided him with a pleasant alternative to a problem from which there seemed no satisfactory solution. Edith accompanied him, and the residence of a year and a half was long enough for him to deepen his knowledge of the country and to advance the studies which he had begun in 1796. Our knowledge of Southey's second visit is far more extensive than for his first because of his long descriptive letters and the journal which he kept of two trips: the first northwards from Lisbon to the university city of Coimbra and the second to the southern province of Algarve as far as the Spanish frontier. The climate of Portugal proved effective in restoring Southey's health – it is quite obvious that his 'nervous' ailment was the result of overwork, an unsettled state of life, and uncertainty over his future. By now he had turned his back upon the law. He had decided upon writing and literature as a career, and he had found that he could earn money and find a place for whatever he chose to write. It was not – and indeed never was to be – a lucrative occupation, but it was what he wanted to do and what he felt himself fitted for. Never in later years did he regret the decision. The warm sun of Portugal, the subtropical splendor of its trees and flowers, the meeting of new people and the stimulation of visiting ancient and picturesque spots in a foreign country – all gave him exactly that change in the pattern of his life which his life in England during the preceding four or five years had been unable to furnish him. Apart from the therapeutic aspect, there were substantial gains. With the encouragement of his uncle he continued his systematic study of Portuguese history and proceeded with his never-completed plan of writing a history of Portugal. There was also time for poetry. The final corrections to *Thalaba* were completed, and the manuscript returned to England, where John Rickman saw to its publication. And since in those days Southey was never without a long narrative poem in hand *The Curse of Kehama* was begun, a romance based upon the Hindoo mythology.

Southey's trip, residence, and travels through Portugal were not without the spice of adventurous risk. The French and English were at war, and the French were placing pressure upon Portugal to drop their old alliance with England and expel the British from their dominions. But the Portuguese were not willing to lose their best market, nor to expose their long and open coastline to the punitive operations of the British fleet. On the five-day voyage from Falmouth, despite the discomforts from sea-sickness there was a moment of excitement and anxiety when an unidentified cutter appeared off the horizon and the ship prepared for a possible exchange of fire. 'Edith, half dead with fear, was stowed in the cockpit – and I stationed myself on the quarter deck with a musquet – which I replaced in the musquet chest with no small joy when the cutter spoke to us – or rather answered us in English' (*New Letters*, vol. 1, p. 224). The French, however, were partially successful at this time in their pressures upon the Portuguese, who, preferring a land to a sea war, declared war upon Spain in February of 1801. The Spanish were successful, and in June by the treaty of Badajoz the regent Dom John gave up Olivenza to the Spanish. Although the Portuguese were stubborn in refusing French demands, the British in Lisbon felt the tension. It was not, however, until long after Southey's departure that the British were forced to leave, and Portugal became for a time a battleground of the Peninsular War. Southey's trip to the south and towards the Spanish frontier was thus attended with some risk. Although Southey and his companion, Samuel Waterhouse, were supplied with passports and letters of introduction, they were the frequent object of suspicion – or at the least curiosity – and of official questioning. Passports were frequently asked for, and at Lagos, soldiers broke into their room at the inn, at midnight and patrolled the doorway for the rest of the night. Although partly or mostly an example of the petty officiousness of the local authorities, the incident illustrated the strictness with which the country was ruled. At Tavira, a town near the border with Spain, the place was filled with soldiers, and only with difficulty did the travellers find accommodation for the night. Despite these irritations – to say nothing of the cold at night, the poor food, the frequent overcharging – Southey's journal is very cheerful. He delighted in the things seen and took a grim interest in such macabre objects as the skeletons to which yellowing flesh still clung. Despite the month of April the weather was cold and often rainy, but there were pleasant days along the sea with a visit to the British consul, John Lemprière, at Faro. However precarious Southey's health may have been in London during the preceding year, his constitution must have recovered remarkably to have endured the considerable hardships of travelling during the winter and spring of 1801. His imperturbability in the presence of many dangers is also notable – the military-political events must be learned from sources other than his journals. It may have been due to a lack of awareness, or it may have been a reflection of the assurance which the free-born Englishman had in his own rights and by virtue of the fact that he was English. A further result of the Portuguese visit was an appreciation of the advantages an Englishman enjoyed. Southey's remark in a letter of May 2, 1800, written soon after his arrival, that 'An Englishman in the streets of Lisbon is like the Heathen Gods of poetry when they descend' (*New Letters*, vol. 1, p. 225) may be somewhat chauvinistic, but it did hold an element of truth.

Southey's time in Portugal had done him a world of good in restoring his health which, from his return in June of 1801 until his final breakdown in the 1830s, seemed to be remarkably stable and enabled him to perform a rigorous schedule of study and writing. Coleridge meanwhile had moved to the Lake District and was settled at Greta Hall in Keswick. In late August the Southeys accepted an invitation to visit the Lakes, which proved rather disappointing after the more spectacular scenery of such places as Cintra in Portugal. Southey was beset by many personal problems, chief of which was a place to live, but decisions had to be made about the education of his brother Henry Herbert and about his mother, whose health was declining. A cousin, Peggy – or Margaret Hill – who lived with his mother was dying of consumption. His own belongings – especially books – were stored at the homes of friends. He also hoped to travel through Wales in order to visit the scenes associated with Madoc, but before all these matters could be attended to Rickman procured for Southey what seemed at first sight a fine opportunity, the secretaryship to Isaac Corry, Chancellor of the Exchequer for Ireland. October found him in Ireland – an entertaining letter to Danvers of October 15 describes the passage across the Irish Sea and arrival in Dublin (*New Letters*, vol. 1, pp. 250–2) – but by November he was back in London. The position proved to be one without many duties and without any future so that Southey resigned in May, 1802 after discovering that Corry really wanted a tutor for his son. The winter of 1801–2 proved unpleasant and was marked by the death of his mother on January 5. She was only fifty-two, but had been suffering from tuberculosis.

Southey spent the rest of the winter of 1802 in London, a city which he continued to dislike, consoling himself with the hope of some secretaryship in the south of Europe. One advantage of the winter in London was the opportunity to meet a variety of persons, some celebrated, and some to become friends or acquaintances in later years. One of these was the historian and lawyer, Sharon Turner; others were the Misses Agnes and Mary Berry, the friends and correspondents of Horace Walpole; Mrs Inchbald, a writer and actress; Mary Hays, an early feminist; the novelist Charlotte Smith; Isaac D'Israeli; the painters John Hoppner and Thomas Lawrence; James Losh from Newcastle; and there was William Godwin whom he sought to avoid because he simply did not enjoy his company. But the chief advantage to the London residence was meeting with some frequency his old friends Bedford, Wynn, John May, and Charles Lamb, together with members of Lamb's circle such as George Dyer. There were also the sights of London, where something was always happening such as the illumination of the French envoy's house, M. Otto, when peace negotiations were concluded.

In September of this year the Southeys' first child was born, a girl named Margaret for his mother, but who was destined to live for only a year. The nagging question during the year had been the persistent one of where to settle and where to find a home. Houses, or houses that he could afford, seemed difficult to find. Now that he had decided upon a literary life the actual place of residence was not of prime importance. At first, he thought of a spot near Richmond, where John May resided, and which would have the advantage of nearness to London and its supply of books, but a suitable house was not found. Later in the summer of 1802 he made a trip to Wales, but was again disappointed. By the end of the year he had returned to Westbury outside of Bristol.

By 1802 Southey was, at the age of twenty-eight, a well-known literary figure. He had published several volumes of short poems, which had gone into more than one edition, a volume of travels, and two long narrative poems *Joan of Arc*, which had gone into a second edition, and *Thalaba*. He had edited the *Annual Anthology* for two years and had contributed anonymously – but anonymity in London was only partially effective – poems to the *Morning Post*, and with the first issue of the *Edinburgh Review* (1802) was given the honor of being hailed as the chief of a new sect of poets who were attacking the orthodox standards of poetry. Jeffrey's attacks were to continue and to increase in severity, but this review of *Thalaba* is not so much an attack upon that work (actually, some good things are conceded to the poem and passages for praise are quoted) as a warning of the dangerous trends in poetry perpetrated by that group to be called shortly the Lake School.

A reading of Southey's letters from his return from Portugal in mid-summer of 1801 to his moving to Keswick two years later reveals a steady and remarkable growth in self-confidence and self-education. The opportunity to learn a language and tradition not his own was one he did not miss. The ambitious plan to write a history of Portugal which he had conceived in Portugal was pursued, and according to statements in his letters about one volume of a projected four-volume work was completed during this period. Some opportunity for translation that would be immediately remunerative came his way in the agreement with Longman to translate *Amadis of Gaul* by Vasco Lobeira for which he received £100. There was reviewing for the newly founded *Annual Review*, edited by Arthur Aikin and also published by Longman, who was now his regular publisher. The pay was not handsome, but it did assist in paying the bills, and Southey worked hard on many of the articles, increasing his knowledge in several areas. He was able to use his knowledge of Spanish and Portuguese literature to good advantage in a ten-page review of A. L. Josse's *El Tesoro Español*. His knowledge of Spanish and Portuguese led him easily into Italian, and here too he was able to review and to translate. Many of his translations of Spanish and Portuguese belong to this period. Substantial reviews of Malthus and of the Methodists made him study and learn of non-literary areas. The residence in Portugal and his readings for the history led him into a study of the monastic orders and to begin a projected – but never completed – history of that subject. These were the years during which Southey began the foundation of his wide learning which enabled him a decade later to be a valued contributor to the *Quarterly* in widely diverse fields of history, literature, biography, and subjects of contemporary social importance. Similarly, many of his friends were also advancing themselves in their careers. John Rickman was establishing himself as a valuable civil servant. Charles Wynn, through the aid of the Wynns and Grenvilles, was increasingly winning his way in politics.

The Southeys left London in May, 1802 for Bristol where they lived for fifteen months as neighbors of his old Bristol friends, Charles Danvers and Danvers' mother. The year, however, brought with it a severe shock to the young couple with the death of their only child, Margaret, during late August. They eagerly accepted the invitation of the Coleridges to visit Greta Hall, where it was thought the company of Edith's sister and the sight of young Sara Coleridge, of the same age as the Southey child, would be helpful. Southey had no way of knowing at the time, but he had made his last journey in search of a home.

Greta Hall was a large house owned by William Jackson and was situated on an eminence with a fine view of mountains and lakes. The house and the view have been described many times, both in prose and poetry, but Charles Lamb's description in September of 1802 describes its appearance when Southey first visited the Lakes.

> He [Coleridge] dwells upon a small hill by the side of Keswick, in a comfortable house, quite enveloped on all sides by a net of mountains: great floundering bears and monsters they seemed,

all couchant and asleep. . . . Coleridge had got a blazing fire in his study; which is a large, antique, ill-shaped room, with an old fashioned organ, never played upon, big enough for a church, shelves of scattered folios, an Aeolian harp, and an old sofa, half-bed, &c. And all looking out upon the last fading view of Skiddaw and his broad-breasted brethren: what a night! (*Letters of Lamb*, vol. 1, p. 315).

Lake Poet and Established Author

When Southey moved to Greta Hall he could not have known how intimately his life would be involved with Coleridge's family. A few months after the arrival of the Southeys, Coleridge left for Malta, where he served as secretary to Sir Alexander Ball. His later visits to Keswick were very short except for his stay of several months during the winter of 1809–10. After 1812 he never returned. In 1803 the Coleridge family was complete: Hartley (born 1796), Derwent (born 1800), and Sara (born 1802). In 1804 Edith May, the first of Southey's seven children to be born at Greta Hall, was born, to be followed by Herbert, Emma, Bertha, Katharine, Isabel, and Cuthbert. Greta Hall was a large three-story house, originally designed as a two-family residence, but in a few years the Southeys seem to have taken it over completely. It was a house filled with children. In addition to the Coleridges and Southeys, the owner, William Jackson, and his house-keeper, Mrs Wilson, had rooms in the house. Jackson died in 1809, but before then Mrs Wilson ('Wilsey' as she was affectionately called) became the servant of the Coleridges and Southeys and played a large part in the upbringing of the children. Southey, despite the demands of authorship, took time to assist in the education of the children, teaching them languages and encouraging them in habits of reading and study. The scholarship of Sara Coleridge, who became a translator and author, is evidence of the thoroughness of his instruction. Mrs Coleridge and Sara continued to live at Greta Hall until 1829 when Sara married her cousin, Henry Nelson Coleridge, both mother and daughter left Greta Hall, their home for over a quarter of a century.

Southey found the first winter cold and uneventful, but conducive to work, since the weather offered little incentive to go outside, and there were few callers. The summer, however, brought a succession of visits from friends, together with strangers who brought letters of introduction. The lakes were fashionable, and if the winter found

Southey cut off from society, the summer made up for the deficiency of the winter. Later he was to complain that the visits and excursions left him little time for writing, and he occasionally had to excuse himself from a party in order to find time for necessary correspondence and composition.

One important consequence of the move to the Lakes was a growing friendship with Wordsworth and his family. Although the two had met as early as 1795 and occasionally thereafter, they had not known each other well. From the time of Southey's arrival at Keswick references to visits are of increasing occurrence, and in later years the children of the households became fast friends and exchanged visits. Mrs Wordsworth's sister, Sarah Hutchinson, was also to become a particular friend and a mainstay in time of trouble. The tragic death of Captain John Wordsworth, William's brother, in the wreck of the *Abergavenny* in February, 1805, brought Wordsworth and Southey together as friends: Wordsworth always remembered the kindness and sympathy of Southey during this bereavement. Dorothy Wordsworth wrote: 'He was so tender and kind that I loved him all at once – he wept with us in our sorrow, and for that cause I think I must always love him.'

The summer of 1805 proved eventful. There were the usual visits from old friends such as Danvers and Duppa (for whom he and Wordsworth did translations for Duppa's book on Michelangelo). And then there was his first trip to Scotland. He was impressed by the beauty and situation of Edinburgh, pleasantly surprised at the urbanity of the diminutive Francis Jeffrey, and quite captivated by Walter Scott. He returned with his prejudices against Scotch Presbyterianism deepened, and he had found Edinburgh a good place to buy books, preferring to bring home books rather than the new coat which he had planned to purchase. 'Edith instructed me to rig myself anew at Edinburgh, with coat, hat, pantaloons, and boots, which I meant to do; but considering that cash was low with me, and that if learning was better than house and land, it certainly must be much better than fine apparel, which is but vanity, I resolved to make the old clothes last till next summer, and accordingly laid out the money at the bookseller's instead of the tailor's!' (November 7, 1805, *Letters*, vol. 1, p. 346).

One evidence of Southey's growing reputation was the confidence which the publishers placed in him. Part of their confidence was their feeling that if he contracted to do a book the work would be forthcoming and would be competently done. Most of his dealings after

1801 were with the firm of Longman – Longman had purchased some of Cottle's titles when Cottle gave up the publishing side of his bookselling business. An interesting project which Longman planned with Southey as manager-in-chief was a Bibliotheca Britannica, a chronological account of English literature – broadly conceived so as to include much more than belles-lettres – with special writers for certain volumes: Turner for Welsh and Saxon; Carlisle for medicine and surgery; Captain Burney for the voyages; Duppa for books on art; Coleridge for the schoolmen; and Rickman as a general assistant in all fields. Longman, however, got cold feet probably worried over the considerable outlay of money and the question of the ultimate profitability of the work, for the project was abandoned three weeks later in August of 1803. It was indeed not until a century later with the appearance of the monumental *Cambridge History of English Literature* that a work of that scope with contributions by a corps of acknowledged specialists realized the plan which Southey outlined – with some counsel from Coleridge and William Taylor. 'Coleridge and I,' he wrote William Taylor, 'have often talked of making a great work upon English Literature.' Southey wrote Wynn:

> The whole plan and arrangement is to be mine and also the choice of associates. It is to be published in parts like the Cyclopaedia, two to a volume, in 4to, 40 lines in a page, 300 pages in a volume. . . . The first part we talk of as to be ready by Xmas 1804 (*New Letters*, vol. 1, p. 319).

The first years of Southey's residence at Keswick passed with little outward incident. His days were occupied with writing and the reading and study that accompanied this writing. His family was growing in number, accompanied by concern over their health and well-being. Almost every year Southey made a trip to London, usually with a circuit of visits either going or returning. In 1806 he made a wide circuit into Norfolk to see William Taylor at Norwich and on his return went into Herefordshire to attend to some of his uncle's business. All Southey's trips were commemorated by minute and detailed descriptions of the places and persons he visited, and these descriptive letters give insights into the life of the times beyond whatever information they may contain for Southey's own life. In 1808 his journey to London was marked by a detour to Bristol, where he had his first meeting with Walter Savage Landor. Landor responded immediately to Southey, and the two became fast friends for the rest of their lives.

When Southey told Landor that he had abandoned the writing of his series of mythological poems – of which *Thalaba* had been the first – because of their inadequate financial return, Landor replied with encouragement: 'Go on with them, and I will pay for printing them, as many as you will write and as many copies as you please.' The result of this offer – which Landor was not called upon to make good – was a resumption of work on *The Curse of Kehama*, which had been laid aside, and the series of letters Southey addressed to Landor, a letter written on long sheets of paper, long enough to include a prose letter as well as the stanzas of *Kehama* that Southey had written. This gesture of encouragement from a fellow-poet meant much to Southey, and he acquired the time for composition by arising early and writing on the poem in the interval before breakfast. This same regimen he followed for *Roderick, the Last of the Goths.*

No account of Southey can be complete without considering him as a bibliophile. His visit to London in 1808 had been largely devoted to the packing of his books, which had received houseroom at Rickman's and Bedford's. Bookshelves had been erected at Greta Hall to house them: one range of shelves along one hallway contained 1,350 volumes. The library continued to grow until it finally reached the impressive total of 14,000 books. Trips to London and other cities usually resulted in additions to his collection. Authors and publishers sent him their books, and the various editors and publishers for whom he wrote normally supplied him with materials. De Quincey, whose first visit to Southey and Greta Hall occurred in 1807, remembered the library of Greta Hall with its panoramic view of mountain and lake and its carefully arranged books – 'fine copies, and decorated externally with a reasonable elegance, so as to make them in harmony with the other embellishments of the room. This effect was aided by the horizontal arrangements upon brackets of many rare manuscripts – Spanish or Portuguese' (*Recollections of the Lake Poets*, ed. E. Sackville-West, 1958, p. 216). Southey had the true collector's regard for his books and took care to preserve as closely as possible their pristine, clean condition. His method of reading and note-taking has been described by his son Cuthbert:

He was as rapid a reader as could be conceived, having the power of perceiving by a glance down the page whether it contained anything which he was likely to make use of – a slip of paper lay on his desk, and was used as a marker, and with a slight pencilled S he would note the passage, put a reference on the paper, with some brief note of the subject, which he could transfer to his note-book, and in the course of a few hours he had classified and arranged everything in the work which it was likely he would ever want (*Life*, vol. 6, pp. 17–18).

These pencilled S's are a valuable clue to books once in Southey's library. An owner who took such pains with his books can hardly be expected to appreciate the friend who borrowed a book, failed to return it, or returned it with heavy underlinings or stains from the butter-knife. Had Southey possessed the fortune and the leisure he might very well have become as great and famous a collector as Richard Heber, who on occasion generously lent some of his books to Southey.

The incidents of Southey's biography can easily become the mere listing of his works together with anecdotes of their composition and the collecting of materials for them. The visit in 1808 to Bristol and the stimulation of his meeting with Landor led him to resume the writing of poetry, but he was finding new direction for his talents in prose, chiefly reviewing. During these years – the first decade of the century – he was accumulating extensive knowledge upon a wide variety of topics, so that in 1809 when he became a regular contributor to the newly founded *Quarterly Review* he had acquired the necessary background and skill in writing reviews; thus he could truly be the 'sheet-anchor' of the *Review* (as Gifford described him) because he was able to write authoritatively on so many assignments that the editor wished competently treated. This task work of his early writing career was thus to be richly rewarded as he turned towards biography and miscellaneous prose.

The first book of prose to show Southey's talent appeared in 1807, the *Letters from England by Don Manuel Alvarez Espriella*, a work ostensibly written by a Spaniard resident in England for a year and a half, and giving a lively picture of many places as well as the habits and customs of English society. Today the social historian finds the book a useful quarry for details of daily life in the period, but the work has also a fictional and autobiographical interest in the persona of Don Manuel, an appealing and sensitively drawn portrait, who often resembles the Englishman Robert Southey. The work is not easy to classify, combining as it does social history, a fictional persona, and many of Southey's own experiences. Anonymous and pseudonymous publication in the early nineteenth century is so common that it seems almost to be the rule rather than the exception. Southey felt that a work known to be by him would receive unfavorable reviews. Although the secret was ill-kept, the work was favorably received, went into a second edition in 1808, and was translated into French and German. Other books to be published in 1808 were largely routine: the *Palmerin of England*, the *Chronicle of the Cid*, and the considerably revised third edition of his *Letters Written in Spain and Portugal*.

Certain years in Southey's life can be seen as turning points. 1803 which saw his establishment of residence at Greta Hall is one. The next notable year is 1809 when his reputation as a writer brought him the opportunity for reasonably lucrative employment: first, as the historian of the *Edinburgh Annual Register*, a new project of Walter Scott and the publishing firm of John Ballantyne; and, second, as a writer for the newly launched *Quarterly Review*, under the editorship of William Gifford and the proprietorship of the publisher John Murray. His friendship with Scott was already paying dividends as Scott was not only the guiding force behind the *Register* but one of the chief advisors of the *Quarterly*. Both the *Register* and the *Quarterly* were established to counterbalance the defeatist attitude of the *Edinburgh Review* towards the Peninsular War and to strengthen the hand of the ministry in its determination to wage the war against Napoleon.

By 1808 the British struggle against Napoleon had been going on for over a decade, and a spirit of discouraged war-weariness and defeatism had seized many Britons, who found in Samuel Whitbread and his followers in Parliament a spokesman and champion, and in the *Edinburgh Review* another voice in Francis Jeffrey, Sydney Smith, and Henry Brougham. When Napoleon sought to subjugate Spain and Portugal, he had not counted upon an uprising of the Spanish and Portuguese peoples, who were experts in guerrilla warfare in their mountainous terrain. The British were not slow in taking advantage of the opportunity to open up a land front, and British forces were sent to the Peninsula to aid the Spaniards. But the move was not greeted with universal approbation by the peace party – those who still sought some accommodation with Napoleon or who felt any struggle was hopeless. Whitbread spoke long and eloquently in Parliament, and the *Edinburgh* in its article, 'Don Cevallos and the French Usurpation in Spain,' derided the efforts of the Spaniards. It was against this spirit that the *Quarterly* and the *Edinburgh Annual Register* spoke out, and not in support of the ministry in all its activities. For

Southey, with his belief in the resolution and fighting capacity of the Spaniards and the knowledge he had gained of the country and of its history and literature, there was a double attraction. And with the renewed interest in all things pertaining to Spain and Portugal Southey was able to turn his knowledge to his own advantage, for now writers on such topics were in demand.

If Southey in the eyes of posterity is the spokesman for reactionary social and political positions, he did not so regard himself. At no time did he think of himself as the tool of the ministry in power, and he never spoke of himself as a Tory. His letter to Grosvenor Bedford (who was the friend of Gifford) when he agreed to become a contributor to the newly founded *Quarterly* expressed his point of view:

> I despise all parties too much to be attached to any. I believe that this country must continue the war while Bonaparte is at the head of France. . . . I am an enemy to any further concessions to the Catholics; I am a friend to the Church establishment. I wish for reform, because I cannot but see that all things are tending towards revolution, and nothing but reform can by any possibility prevent it (*Life*, III, 183–184).

The proprietors and advisers of the *Quarterly* were by no means willing to trust him with the expression of official governmental views. When the first issue of the review appeared in February 1809, the leading article on Affairs in Spain was the joint production of George Ellis and George Canning, the latter of whom was to become Prime Minister. Southey's essay in this first number was a defence of the Baptist Missionary Society, a reply to a derisive review in the *Edinburgh* on the same topic, but Scott had four essays, one of which was a courteous review of Southey's recently published translation of the *Chronicle of the Cid*. It is not until 1811 that Southey begins to write on political matters, and when he was entrusted with the review of Captain Pasley's *Military Policy of Great Britain*, a popular book urging aggressive action against France, the article was so thoroughly rewritten by Croker that Southey disclaimed its authorship. In his 'History of the Year' for the first four volumes of the *Edinburgh Annual Register* (1808–11 – but published always two years after the events described) Southey had a free hand in which to express his faith in the power of the Spanish people to overthrow the grievous and hateful oppression of Napoleon, as well as to express his views of those Members of Parliament such as Whitbread who had kinder words for the French and Napoleon than for their brave allies. In addition to the events of the war, Southey also commented upon matters domestic and in general was favorable to humanitarian reforms. Much of the *Register*, of course, was factual and descriptive, but it is still within the pages of these four volumes that the reader can find the fullest expression of Southey's views during the years of the struggle against Napoleon. By working within the existing framework of government many reforms, Southey believed, could be achieved such as the improvement of the condition of the poor, the support of Christian missions, and plans for national education.

The winter of 1811–12 brought Southey an interesting encounter with a young man who first approached him as a disciple looking for a master. The visitor was Percy Bysshe Shelley, newly married, and fresh from his expulsion at Oxford and the authorship of his pamphlet *The Necessity of Atheism*. Southey was by no means shocked at this flouting of academic authority, nor even at an early – and what many might have called an imprudent – marriage. For had he had not been guilty of the same things? Shelley, he wrote, 'is brimful and over-flowing with everything good and generous – tho the Oxford men were as much shocked at him as if he had had hoofs and horns, four and forty iron teeth, and a tail with a sting at the end of it' (*New Letters*, vol. 2, p. 20n). It is tempting to make a close parallel between Southey and Shelley, however divergent their views and careers as well as life-styles were to be. Southey thought he saw in Shelley an image of himself at nineteen, although at the time of their meeting he was twice Shelley's age. There was a similarity in voice, in the incidents of early life – expulsion from school for a school composition, an early marriage, an estrangement from some family members, a great desire to better the condition of the world, a genuine devotion to poetry – it is indeed no wonder that Southey responded to Shelley, but his own disillusioned middle age was not able long to respond to Shelley's ebullient spirits and to his rather quixotic attempts to reform society: Shelley's own disillusionment was to come later and in different form, but that is Shelley's story and not Southey's. By the time the Shelleys left Keswick for Ireland Shelley was disappointed to find that Southey and he did not agree on so many issues, but Southey had seen enough to predict that Shelley would be a major figure. The two men never met again, and each moved in different circles and circles hostile to each other. In 1816 Shelley sent Southey a copy of *Alastor*. In 1818 Shelley was told that Southey had written attacks upon him in reviews of Hunt's *Foliage* and his own *Revolt of Islam* and again wrote Southey. The demand for information was couched in outwardly civil form, and Southey disclaimed the authorship of the reviews (which seem to have been by John T. Coleridge) and asserted that he had never referred to Shelley in any of his writings. The correspondence ended on a somewhat polite tone, but the differences between the two were considerable. Southey on his part had received information or gossip about Shelley's life in Italy (it may have come through Landor whom he visited in Italy in 1817 or, more likely, from John T. Coleridge or J. W. Croker) so that long after Shelley's death Southey could write in harsh – and disappointed – terms that 'the story is the most frightful tragedy that I have ever known in real life' (*New Letters*, vol. 2, p. 474).

1813 was another eventful year in Southey's life. His most highly praised and most frequently reprinted book, *The Life of Nelson*, appeared, expanded at John Murray's suggestion from a *Quarterly* article into a book. Later in the year he received the appointment of Poet Laureate, rather ironically as he was turning away more and more from poetry to prose. The letters of Southey and Scott are the best source of information concerning the behind-the-scenes manoeuvering of this appointment, but the story seems to be that Scott first received the offer, turned it down partly because he felt he already had received sufficient preferment and emoluments from the public, and also because he felt that the office had fallen into such disrepute. Scott, on refusing the offer, recommended Southey, who accepted it with the expectation that the requirement of odes on set occasions would be abolished. Nothing, however, was officially done so that Southey had often to fulfil requests from the court composers, Sir William Parsons and William Shields, to provide texts for musical compositions. Southey raised the post into respectability partly because he was the first poet in a century of any stature or reputation who had ever held the laureateship. Afterwards Wordsworth and Tennyson were not ashamed to be named to the post, nor was Leigh Hunt in 1843 ashamed to pull strings in order to secure the post for himself. In the twentieth century the laureate has generally been a poet of the first rank, but no longer is he expected to produce – except as he may feel himself compelled to do so – verses on demand. One of the best of Southey's laureate poems is his first, 'Carmen Triumphale, For the Commencement of the Year 1814' – 'a vigorous and on the whole successful piece' judges Kenneth Hopkins (*The Poets Laureate*, London, 1954, p. 138). His most unfortunate – and in some ways most widely known – is, of course, his *Vision of Judgment*, a poem demanded by the death of George III only to be brilliantly satirized by Byron in his own *Vision* of the same event. The stipend of the laureateship was modest but Southey invested the proceeds in an insurance policy for his family. Indeed, the small emolument from the office was not unimportant to him.

Southey's family had increased steadily since 1803 when he settled at Keswick. By 1813 he had five children: Edith May, born in 1804; Herbert in 1806; Bertha in 1809; Katharine in 1810; and Isabel in 1812 (Emma, born in 1808, had lived only fifteen months). All these as well as the large house of Greta Hall must be supported by the activity of his pen. Although Southey was concerned over what he called ways and means, he kept his anxieties largely to himself. He found his role as father and head of the household a congenial one. He loved and enjoyed the company of children, as his letters to his own children (and to Hartley Coleridge) testify: these letters must rank among the best ever penned to children. He had the ability to respond to their interests, take them very seriously, and never condescend. The one immortal classic that came from Southey's pen – based, he said, upon a story told him by his eccentric uncle William Tyler – was a by-product of this love for his own children – The Story of the Three Bears – which he ultimately gave to the world in 1837 in *The Doctor*. His second daughter became known as Bertha Bruin, and evidence that his young cousins, the sons of his uncle Herbert Hill, also knew the story can be seen in the nicknames awarded them.

He writes to his wife in 1813 of his visit to the Hills and of the Hill children: 'Below stairs the young Bears put all my accomplishments in requisition. . . . I am a huge favourite with two of these young ones and have raised all three to the peerage, in honour of the parts they bear by similitude in their favourite story by the names of Duke Bruin, Marquis Bruin, and Earl Bruin – so you may give Bertha a kiss and tell her that her Welsh Uncles are all Bruins as well as herself. . . . Yesterday after dinner I told the story of the Three Bears with universal applause' (*New Letters*, vol. 2, pp. 79, 72, 67).

Southey's happy household life was broken, however, in 1816 with the death of his only son, Herbert, after an illness of several weeks. This child, only ten years old, gave evidence of a quick native intelligence and great aptitude for study, which his father encouraged, often acting as his son's tutor especially in languages. Of the many letters which he wrote announcing the event to his closest friends all are painful to read, and one excerpt from many may suffice. Two days after the event Southey wrote Grosvenor Bedford on April 18:

> Wherefore do I write to you? Alas, because I know not what to do. . . . To-day I hope I shall support myself, or rather that God will support me, for I am weak as a child, in body even more than in mind. My limbs tremble under me; long anxiety has wasted me to the bone, and I fear it will be long before grief will suffer me to recruit. I am seriously apprehensive for the shock which my health seems to have sustained; yet I am wanting in no effort to appear calm and to console others; and those who are about me give me credit for a fortitude which I do not possess. Many blessings are left me. . . . I have strong ties to life, and many duties yet to perform. . . . It is some relief to write to you, after the calls which have this day been made upon my fortitude. . . . Never, perhaps, was child of ten years old so much to his father. Without ever ceasing to treat him as a child, I had made him my companion, as well as playmate and pupil, and he had learnt to interest himself in my pursuits, and take part in all my enjoyments (*Life*, vol. 4, pp. 161–4).

In time the sorrow and depression were mitigated, but Southey had learned a lesson that he should not give his heart and affections so unreservedly to a child, whose life was so precarious. From this severe blow Southey never quite recovered.

The condition of England, too, in 1816 was not cheerful. The historian Wingfield-Stratford has declared: 'The state of hopeless misery into which the country was plunged in the black year 1816 baffles description.' Although 1815 and Napoleon's defeat at Waterloo had brought an end to over two decades of war and threats to national security from the French forces of Napoleon, external troubles were only exchanged for grave internal problems. The wartime prosperity had extended to many classes of society, but peace brought a decline in the price of corn, much agricultural distress, and correspondingly depressed prices in manufacturing. Many who had enjoyed profits from farming and business found themselves facing financial ruin. Unemployment was widespread, bankruptcies were increasing, and there was much talk of radical movements. The ministerial party approached Southey to write in its behalf, and in 1817 he was offered the editorship of *The Times*, an offer which he declined, but he was turning his attention to the problems of society such as the spread of inflammatory seditious writing, distress among the poor and un-employed, national education, the need for reforms in the law and in the franchise. On these matters he was by no means the spokesman of the ministers or of any one particular group. He spoke out on such diverse topics as education, the poor laws and the poor, emigration, the Roman Catholic question and Ireland, the moral and political state of the nation. A summing up of his views is most conveniently seen in his *Colloquies on the Progress and Prospects of Society*, published in 1829, and in *Essays, Moral and Political* (1832).

Southey's basic outlook on life was cheerful, his interests varied, his confidence in himself to do what the situation demanded complete, but after 1816 there is certainly a less cheerful note, an anxiety for the welfare of the state, and some anxiety over his own ability to meet the demands that might in the future be placed upon him. This change in attitude was at first the result of the death of Herbert, but it could not but be intensified by the depression in which England was plunged in the post-war years. Increasingly, Southey feared for the safety of the state and thought that revolution and rebellion were not far away. The fact that his worst fears were unrealized does not deny the existence of the fears, which were by no means his alone but were generally shared by the public. The repressive actions of the government, how-ever questionable in the eyes of posterity, were an understandable response to the threats and dangers of the day.

Southey had been increasingly the target of journalistic abuse, most of it politically inspired. His acceptance of the laureateship had been the signal for stepped-up attacks by writers who found in him a con-venient way to attack the ministry for its shortcomings. The terms of turncoat, renegade, and apostate were freely used, and however un-just, greatly influenced the regard in which Southey was held in his own day and have continued into the twentieth century – in the same way that Browning's poem 'The Lost Leader' still unfortunately clings to the reputation of Wordsworth. They are convenient tags with which to label writers with simplistic judgments. The earliest attacks upon Southey came from Francis Jeffrey, first in the *Monthly Review*, and later in the first issue of the *Edinburgh Review*, where he was bracketed with Wordsworth and Coleridge as a leader in a dangerous new cult of poetry. Thereafter, the *Edinburgh* seldom spoke of Southey except in derision or disparagement. Lesser reviewers, usually anony-mous, often assailed Southey as his reputation and list of publications increased. He occasionally sought to publish anonymously thinking by that means to avoid the censure that would almost automatically be bestowed upon a work to which his name was attached. Francis Jeffrey and the *Edinburgh* were Whig in politics, and when Southey became a regular contributor to the *Quarterly*, he was then throwing in his lot with the ministerial party, and became a fair target for all writers in the opposition. In addition to Jeffrey, who was the spokesman for the respectable and established opposition, new assailants appeared in the persons of Leigh Hunt and William Hazlitt, writers of the extreme radical opposition. Their reviews and attacks appeared chiefly in Hunt's *Examiner* and the *Morning Chronicle*. How frequently Southey saw and read these periodicals is hard to determine, but he was certainly informed on occasion of the attacks, and he grew increasingly bitter towards these writers for their unfairness and what he felt in Hazlitt was a personal (and unjustified) animosity. Wordsworth too shared in this feeling towards his detractors, and both felt that the sustained attacks on themselves personally and on their works for over a decade seriously lowered the sales of their books. The attacks meant also that Southey was cut off from the esteem and influence he might have had upon the younger generation of writers. Keats, Shelley, and Byron all at some time admired and even imitated some of Southey's poems, but their ultimate judgment of him was negative. The attacks upon Southey began with Jeffrey's review of *Thalaba* in the *Edinburgh* for 1802, reached a crescendo in the second decade of the century with the attacks of Hunt and Hazlitt, and came to a final climax in Byron's witty and devastating *Vision of Judgment*. A later attack came some ten years later in 1830 with Macaulay's review of the *Colloquies* in the *Edinburgh*. These continued attacks, with what Southey thought to be a carefully laid and concerted plan of action, must have had an adverse effect upon the sale of his works: certainly many of Southey's ill-natured and querulous references to his critics can easily be understood not only in terms of wounded pride but as also coming from a writer whose very livelihood depended upon the sale of his works. Not until 1835 was Southey able to say that he was a year ahead in his personal expenses.

In March of 1817 the most irritating attack came with the piratical publication of *Wat Tyler*, a play with French revolutionary principles which Southey had hurriedly written during the summer of 1794, had left with Ridgeway and Symonds to publish, but when it had not been printed had forgotten. By means never revealed the manuscript of this work fell into the hands of a person who had the work published by Sherwood, Neely, and Jones. The political opposition fell with delight upon this youthful indiscretion, and William Smith read in the House of Commons excerpts from the play with contrasting sentences from the *Quarterly Review*. Charles Wynn answered on behalf of his friend, and Southey went so far as to write a long answer in defense of himself in a pamphlet, *A Letter to William Smith, Esq. M.P.* On the advice of his friends Southey sought an injunction against the publication of the pamphlet, but Lord Eldon denied the injunction on the rather curious ground that a work designed to injure society could not receive the protection of the laws of that society.

Last Years

The last two decades of Southey's life – roughly the 1820s and 1830s – saw many political, social, and economic changes. Many political changes such as the moves for Catholic Emancipation and the agitation for the Reform Bill he viewed with dismay, but such humanitarian movements as the humanization of the penal code, education for the masses, savings banks, and emigration to the colonies he warmly advocated. Under the leadership of George Canning during the 1820s and of Robert Peel during the 1830s, many changes in both foreign and domestic policies occurred. Under Canning, British support for the despotic governments of Russia and Austria lessened, and such causes as Greek independence received official support. At home Peel as Home Secretary abandoned the system of espionage among working men and prosecution of the press. The death penalty was repealed for many offences, and a series of legal reforms dealing with the entrenched habits of procrastination in the law courts was begun. An important service of Peel came in 1829 with the establishment of the metropolitan police force to replace the inept and outdated system of the old watch. Had such a force been in existence in 1819 the Peterloo Massacre might well have been averted. After Canning's death in 1827 the new government led by Wellington saw a series of reform measures pass Parliament, including the repeal of the Test Act, which had excluded dissenters from holding national and municipal offices. The repeal of the restrictions against Roman Catolics was more difficult, tied as it was to the emotional problem of Ireland, but Peel and Wellington recognized that the time had come, and the bill passed in 1828. Southey's opposition to concessions to the Roman Catholics was emotional and deep-seated, but his feeling was certainly shared by the majority of his countrymen in whom the spirit of 'no popery' was firmly rooted. In 1832 the Reform Bill passed, extending the franchise and doing something to equalize the basis of representation in Parliament. The reform was very modest, and neither the worst fears nor highest expectations of opponent or advocate were realized: an opening, however, for a wider electorate had been made, and the first of a series of extensions that was to reach into the twentieth century had started.

The mood of the nation during the decade of the 1820s was one of fear – fear of change and of civil war. Britain was no longer actively involved in Continental affairs as it had been during the war against Napoleon, but in 1830 a potentially disturbing situation arose when the French deposed Charles IX and replaced him with Louis-Philippe as a constitutional monarch very much upon the British model. The despotic powers threatened war over this change, troops were assembled upon the frontier, and Britons feared an involvement in a new Continental war. These fears were intensified by outbreaks of local violence, but the danger passed. The tension created, however, by this new French revolution, coupled with the distressing poverty of many Englishmen and a rapidly threatening and deteriorating situation in Ireland served to hasten the passage of the Reform Bill two years later.

But if political movements at home and abroad occupied the center of the stage, technological changes were taking place that would profoundly affect the daily lives of everyone. In 1830 a railway between Liverpool and Manchester was opened, and in a very few years, a network of railway lines traversed the island, bringing the end for the picturesque stagecoach with its long, fatiguing journeys. After Waterloo the British colonies received a steady number of emigrants, individuals and families who had found it difficult to make their way in the old country: Canada, South Africa, Australia, and New Zealand provided a home for these new settlers. Unplanned, this movement contributed to the building of the empire, and Southey welcomed it as a means of improving the lot of individuals and relieving the pressures at home of a growing population. Progress continued in providing education for the masses of the people, efforts were made to improve conditions in prisons, and similar efforts were begun for a more humane treatment of those in mental hospitals. In 1833 the work of the abolitionists such as Wilberforce and Clarkson was crowned with success with the passage of the law ending slavery in the British possessions. For this Southey rejoiced.

During these years of important national and international changes Southey's own life was almost totally devoted to authorship. Despite the attacks of the radical press, and the disappointing sale of his books, his services as a writer were in demand and he could sell his work at a satisfactory, if not a high, price. The *Quarterly* was his steadiest and most constant source of income, but with the advent of John G. Lockhart as editor in 1826, he wrote less and less for that review. From time to time recurring financial distress in the nation was felt by authors and booksellers, and although the houses of Murray and Longman stood firm when the Constables and Ballantynes were failing, book sales were affected by the economy, and publishing ventures were not always profitable. Southey's name had sufficient strength – in the eyes of publisher and editor – to carry off at least an edition or two. The list of such ventures during these last years of Southey's authorial life is impressive testimony to his reputation. In 1820 appeared his *Life of Wesley*. In 1824 came *The Book of the Church*, designed as a popular history of the Church of England, and a title that a publisher might hope would be a steady seller on his back-list; and in 1833, the first of his lives of the British Admirals for Lardner's *Cabinet Cyclopaedia* – an obvious subject for the author of the popular biography of Nelson. He introduced an edition of Bunyan's *Pilgrim's Progress* (1830) with a biography of Bunyan, which was embellished with many engravings and illustrations. An anthology, *British Poets from Chaucer to Jonson*, appeared in 1831. And finally from 1835 to 1837 one of his most interesting and impressive editorial and biographical labors, *The Works of William Cowper . . . With a Life of the Author*, was written. This biography is still readable, and the sketch of literary history is a valuable document for the way in which the writers of the age viewed their literary predecessors. These works were done by contract, and Southey was approached by the publishers, who, it must be said, often had a better idea of the commercial possibilities of his work than did Southey himself.

During the summer of 1826 a curious and unexpected event occurred. On Southey's return from a summer trip to the Netherlands he discovered that Lord Radnor had returned him as a Member of Parliament for the borough of Downton. The residents of Keswick, feeling that the town had been greatly honored, were assembled to greet their new celebrity. Lord Radnor, who knew Southey only by reputation, had acted without consulting him, and Southey, who had no wish for a political career, declined the election. His letters indicate that he was amused by the incident, somewhat bothered by the technical difficulties of refusing the election, and profiting to the extent that letters addressed to him – in those days the recipient had to pay the postage – came without the customary charges. With characteristic scrupulosity, however, he did not avail himself of the franking privilege for his own correspondence while he was technically an M.P.

The summer of 1826, although diverted by this parliamentary election, was saddened by the severe illness of his daughter Isabel, a girl in her fourteenth year. Her illness grew worse, and she died on July 16. Although this unexpected death was a shock to the father, it did not equal that caused by the death of his son Herbert ten years earlier. But Mrs Southey, who had been in declining health and spirits, did not recover from the shock of this death, and her physical and mental health gradually worsened until eight years later in 1834 she had to be committed to the Retreat, a hospital at York conducted by Quakers. In 1835 she had recovered to the extent that she could be returned home, although she never regained her reason. Her death came on November 16, 1837.

The years had brought other changes. In 1829 Sara Coleridge married her cousin Henry Nelson Coleridge, and Sara and her mother left Greta Hall. In 1834 Edith May Southey married the Reverend John Wood Warter and left to make her home in West Tarring, Sussex. The family circle at Greta Hall was narrowing, and Southey remained in his study more and more, breaking his routine by a long daily walk in all weather and at every season. Mrs Southey's health made it impossible for the family to entertain house guests. In 1828 the Reverend Herbert Hill died, and Southey paid his final tribute to his memory by a poem affixed to his *Sir Thomas More; Or, Colloquies on the Progress and Prospects of Society*. A fancied resemblance between his uncle and the Holbein portrait of More provided an excuse for dedicating the work to his uncle's memory.

Southey's friendships were formed for the most part during the early years of his life, and although there was a falling off with many of these as distance, changing interests, and differences of temperament became more apparent, there were also some new friends. Southey's interest in the poetry of Henry Kirke White, whose poetical remains he edited (1808) and which became a modest best-seller, resulted in his friendship with Neville White, brother of Henry and a clergyman. Neville White was a frequent visitor and was the companion of Southey on his trip to the Netherlands in 1825. Henry Taylor (later

Sir Henry) was, according to Southey's own testimony, his best friend among the younger generation. Henry Taylor began a literary career by his verse tragedies *Isaac Comnenus* (1827) and *Philip van Artevelde* (1834). His later career was at the Colonial Office, but he also wrote reviews for the *Quarterly*. He was appointed literary executor by Southey's will, but he did not edit any of Southey's remains, nor did he write the biography which it was assumed he would. Taylor was also a visitor to Keswick and accompanied Southey on his trip to Holland in 1826.

Southey lived long enough to witness the deaths of his contemporaries. In 1832 Scott died, and in 1834 both Coleridge and Lamb. The old intimacy with Coleridge had long been over, but the death was affecting since his own life had been so inextricably woven with Coleridge's, and some of Coleridge's problems had perforce become his own. He said little on the occasion, but it was never his habit to indulge in sentimental reminiscence or lament for what might have been.

The most significant friendship of Southey's middle and later years was with Caroline Bowles, who became in 1839 the second Mrs Southey. She first approached Southey with a request for criticism of her work and for assistance in finding a publisher. Southey's first letter to her (*New Letters*, vol. 2, pp. 189–91) was dated August 12, 1818 and consisted of a minute criticism of her poem *Ellen Fitzarthur* on the premise that 'criticism cannot be too minute nor too rigid when it is in time to prevent what is faulty from being rendered permanent by the press.' His conclusion was encouraging: 'Be of good heart, and whatever may be the fate of this poem, do not be discouraged from planning and executing thus.' Longman later published the poem after Murray refused. The correspondence so begun continued. Alone in the world, Caroline Bowles was then thirty-two and lived modestly in a small house at Buckland near Lymington. She was seeking by authorship to augment her meager income. She was the daughter of a captain in the service of the East India Company and a niece of General Sir Harry Burrard, whose son Paul is the subject of Southey's inscription 'To the Memory of Paul Burrard.' Southey first met Miss Bowles in London during the summer of 1820. In late 1823 she visited Keswick, and from that time the friendship and correspondence grew. Southey suggested that they collaborate upon a poem about Robin Hood, a project which never proceeded beyond a few stanzas. Southey's first visit to Buckland occurred during the winter of 1824 on his fifteen-week trip to London and the West of England. Other visits followed, and Southey found that he was able to finish writing assignments for the *Quarterly* at Buckland without the interference of London and its social demands. Edward Dowden's edition of *The Correspondence of Robert Southey with Caroline Bowles* (1881) provides a complete account of this friendship, and a quotation from Dowden's rather old-fashioned Victorian prose indicates what this relationship meant to each. For Caroline Bowles, Dowden wrote:

> It is impossible to estimate how much she gained of hope and vigour from Southey's personal presence and from his kind and constant communication by the pen. Without him her life would have narrowed and dwindled and grown grey. With him for her friend, the world always owned one thing which made life a valuable possession.

On Southey's side, and in explanation of his proposal of marriage, Dowden further wrote:

> When, after change and grievous loss in his home . . . when he dared to look forward to a quiet eventide of toil, he found that his friend of twenty years, whose age approached his own, and whose sympathy with his thoughts and strivings was constantly and instinctively right, would be the truest and most helpful companion for the close of life. Making no breach with the past, he might draw the bonds of their friendship tighter; he might perfect that friendship in the dearest way of all (p. xxiii).

Caroline Bowles's poems and tales in verse enjoyed a modest popularity during her day, and her lachrymose and pathetic tales – occasionally of the sufferings of children under the conditions of child labor – suited the taste of many readers. In addition to her publications in book form, the annuals and *Blackwood's* provided other outlets for her writing.

The years of Southey's life after 1834 were, if possible, increasingly quiet and more devoted than ever to writing and study. He still thought of completing his history of Portugal and of doing a history of the monastic orders, but assignments from booksellers, including the preparation of the ten-volume edition of his collected poetry to which he wrote informative prefaces, occupied his hours at the desk. His health continued good until apparently the end of 1837. Persons, however, who had not seen him for several years noticed a difference. The American Hispanic scholar, George Ticknor, who had not seen

Southey since 1819 wrote: 'Southey was natural and kind, but evidently depressed, much altered since I saw him fifteen years ago, a little bent, and his hair quite white.'

There are few events to record for these last few years. In 1835 Sir Robert Peel offered Southey a baronetcy, and although he appreciated the honor, he declined since, among other reasons, he had not the fortune to maintain such a position. His dignified and manly reply to Peel for the generosity of his offer stated fully and frankly his financial situation, the mental illness of his wife, and his fears that he might by 'a sudden stroke' be deprived 'of those faculties, by the exercise of which this poor family has hitherto been supported.' The result of this exchange was the award of a pension of £300, a desire on Peel's part to recognize literary achievement, and for the first time in his forty years as an author Southey was relieved of any uneasiness over a proper provision for his family and himself.

In addition to the various reviews and books of these years, the most notable incident was the long journey from October, 1836 to February, 1837 in which Southey, accompanied by Cuthbert, then a youth of seventeen, visited Bristol and the haunts of his youth. Very few of those he had once known were still alive or resident there, but he did visit the Cottles, saw Landor for the last time, and went on to Helston in Cornwall, where Mrs Coleridge was residing with her son Derwent. On the return from the West of England there was a further visit to Miss Bowles at Buckland and stops in London to see Henry Herbert Southey and John Rickman. The visit was on the whole a great success, and Southey's letters describing the stages of the journey are full of the minutiae of places visited, persons seen, and the incidents along the way. In the summer of 1838 he took his final vacation trip, this time a trip to France, in the company of H. C. Robinson, Humphry Senhouse, John Kenyon, Cuthbert, and Kenyon's friend Captain Jones. The journal which he kept marks a noticeable falling off in his mental powers, a decline that his companions also observed. Robinson sadly noted: 'He had lost all power of conversation, and seldom spoke' (Henry Crabb Robinson, *On Books and Their Writers*, 1938, vol. 2, p. 556).

Prior to this departure for France, Southey had a last visit with Carlyle and warmly praised the *French Revolution*, just published in 1837. Carlyle commented: 'My poor *French Revolution* evidently appeared to him a Good Deed, a salutary bit of "scriptural" exposition for the public and mankind.'

Despite his failing powers and depression of spirits Southey continued at the writing desk, planned to get on with his unfinished projects, and completed his last review for the *Quarterly*, a life of Thomas Telford, the engineer, in whose company he had visited Scotland in 1819. Early in 1838 his daughter Bertha married her cousin Herbert Hill, Jr. Southey's own marriage to Caroline Bowles took place on June 4, 1838. But his mind and memory were rapidly failing, and by November the total failure of his faculties was evident to all. When Wordsworth called during the summer of 1840, Southey did not recognize him. But Southey lived on until March 21, 1843. The last years were melancholy ones for the Southey family, and it was well that Southey himself was spared the dissension which arose between the second Mrs Southey and Kate Southey. Sides were taken. The Warters, Henry Herbert Southey, and Landor supported Caroline, but the Hills (Bertha Southey), Cuthbert, and the Wordsworths supported Kate Southey. The dissension persisted after Southey's death and resulted in the inability of Henry Taylor, the best qualified of all Southey's friends, to edit a selection of letters and write a biography. Cuthbert Southey's six-volume *Life and Correspondence of the Late Robert Southey* and the four-volume edition of *Letters* by J. W. Warter are visible evidences of this rift. After the death of Southey, Mrs Southey returned to Hampshire where she lived quietly until her death in 1854.

A biographical account of Southey's life and career may fittingly conclude by quoting Wordsworth's 'Inscription for a Monument in Crosthwaite Church, in the Vale of Keswick':

Ye vales and hills whose beauty hither drew
The poet's steps, and fixed him here, on you
His eyes have closed! And ye, lov'd books, no more
Shall Southey feed upon your precious lore,
To works that ne'er shall forfeit their renown,
Adding immortal labours of his own –
Whether he traced historic truth, with zeal
For the State's guidance, or the Church's weal,
Or Fancy, disciplined by studious art,
Inform'd his pen, or wisdom of the heart,
Or judgments sanctioned in the Patriot's mind
By reverence for the rights of all mankind.
Wide were his aims, yet in no human breast
Could private feelings meet for holier rest.

His joys, his griefs, have vanished like a cloud
From Skiddaw's top; but he to heaven was vowed
Through his industrious life, and Christian faith
Calmed in his soul the fear of change and death.

Literary Friendships

Southey either met or had some kind of interesting connection with
almost every literary man of his time. With Coleridge, Wordsworth,
Lamb, Scott, and Landor the relationship was far more than casual,
and for Shelley and Byron, the association has become an interesting
chapter in their biographies. For many others such as Keats and Blake,
the connection is hardly more than a footnote. For Carlyle and Charlotte Brontë, the relationship consisted of encouragement and advice
at the beginning of their careers. For a host of writers of the second
and third stature – such as William Taylor, James Montgomery, John
G. Lockhart – the allusions in Southey's correspondence must suffice.

The earliest man of letters with whom Southey became intimate –
and his first encounter with an authentic man of genius – was Coleridge
whom he met in 1794 when he was twenty and Coleridge twenty-two.
This friendship is the most difficult of all Southey's friendships to
assess. After Coleridge left Keswick in 1812 and the break with Mrs
Coleridge became complete, the two saw very little of each other.
Biographers of Coleridge defend Coleridge in most matters and see
Southey to blame for the falling away, and biographers of Southey
defend Southey. But it is not a profitable exercise. To assess the relationship between the two it is not really necessary to decide degrees of
fault. There were deep-seated differences in temperament and habits
of life evident from the beginning of their friendship in 1794. Southey
at the age of twenty was already leading an orderly, well-organized
existence and appears to have adhered rather steadily to a schedule,
whereas Coleridge did not. A clash between two such temperaments
was inevitable sooner or later, especially when the two persons shared
the same rooms and saw each other daily. Despite the differences in
years, the younger Southey had a more realistic concept of goals, and,
although he had worked hard in setting pantisocracy into motion, he
realized the impossibility of ever finding the funds needed. There were
also mischiefmakers among the friends of each who were willing to
tell tales that were better left untold. In 1797–9 Charles Lloyd was one
such, and William Hazlitt, who was the friend of neither Southey nor

Coleridge, printed sarcastic remarks Coleridge was said to have made
about Southey in a public house, and Southey felt that certain persons –
Wade and Gilman – close to Coleridge in later years were quick to
fault him. But despite all quarrels, harsh words, and reconciliations,
there remained a mutual respect for the achievements of each. The
public pronouncements on the whole were generous, especially
the third chapter of *Biographia Literaria* in which Coleridge gave to the
world what he wished it to know about Southey. These words were
deliberate, they did not have to be said, and should weigh more
heavily than irritable chance words thrown off in a letter or a conversation. Southey, despite the assertions of some biographers and scholars,
exerted himself to help Coleridge. The recently published (1965) new
letters of Southey give abundant testimony to his efforts to secure
employment for Coleridge in the *Quarterly* and to review his works
in that periodical. These efforts were unsuccessful, but their joint
Omniana (1812) was an attempt to gain employment and recompense
for Coleridge. In 1809 he solicited subscriptions for Coleridge's *Friend*.
His very real and daily efforts on behalf of Coleridge's family cannot
be praised too highly. Without the assistance of Southey and Wordsworth, who literally begged the money from Coleridge's family and
friends, Hartley could never have gone to college. The Coleridge
children were, of course, the cousins of his own children, but the
generous and unqualified tributes of both Sara and Hartley testify to
the goodness of Southey towards them, and his tact in fulfilling a
difficult role. Hartley Coleridge phrased it very neatly and revealingly:
'Now if you want to make a man hated, hold him up as an Example.
It is an extraordinary proof of the loveliness of Southey's character,
that though his name was rife in every objurgation and every admoni-
tion I received, I never could help but love him' (*Letters*, ed. G. E. and
E. L. Griggs, London, 1936, p. 186).

The friendship between Southey and Wordsworth was unruffled
by any dispute. The incidents of this friendship can be quickly narrated.
Although the two had met in the 1790s and were known to each
other through Coleridge and other friends, the intimacy between the
two men and their families did not develop until after Southey's
residence in Keswick in 1803. Southey's kindness to the Wordsworths
at the time of John Wordsworth's drowning at the wreck of the
Abergavenny in 1805 marked the deepening of the friendship. Southey
had early recognized Wordsworth's greatness as a poet, but Wordsworth had reservations about Southey's poetry and preferred his prose.

The early poems of Southey are often written in the same style and use the same subjects that Wordsworth made famous in *Lyrical Ballads*. In 1807 the two contributed translations to Richard Duppa's biography of Michelangelo, and in 1809 the two worked together on a petition concerning the infamous Convention of Cintra. In 1819 Wordsworth dedicated *Peter Bell* to Southey, and in the year before both were involved in the election for Westmorland, in which Henry Brougham attacked both Wordsworth and Southey from the hustings. As the Southey and Wordsworth children grew up, the visits between the two households increased, and Edith May Southey and Dora Wordsworth became the best of friends.

Southey's friendship with Scott began in 1805 when Southey first visited Scotland. Earlier, he had reviewed Scott's *Sir Tristrem* in the *Annual Review*, and Scott for his part had reviewed Southey's *Amadis*. In 1805 Scott was at the beginning of his fame, for his first success, *The Lay of the Last Minstrel*, had just appeared. The two shared so many interests – prominent among these was a knowledge of medieval romances and of Spanish literature – that a literary friendship was almost certain to develop. Scott's generosity to fellow-poets was early exhibited: in 1807 he invited Southey to review for the *Edinburgh*, and later secured his services for the *Quarterly* at its founding in 1809, and in the same year he also enrolled Southey as the writer of the historical section for the *Edinburgh Annual Register*, one of the projects of the firm of John Ballantyne and Company. Scott's efforts to secure a governmental post or a professorship were not successful. In 1813 when Scott was offered the laureateship he declined the honor, wrote to J. W. Croker recommending Southey, and urged Southey in turn to accept. Scott held a high regard for Southey as a man and praised his work highly in public, but privately he thought that Southey in his poetry was 'often diffuse, and frequently sets much value on minute and unimportant facts, and useless pieces of abstruse knowledge' (*Journal*, ed. W. E. K. Anderson, 1972, p. 19). To Byron, however, he wrote: 'He is a real poet, such as we read of in former times, with every atom of his soul and every moment of his time dedicated to literary pursuits' (*Letters of Scott*, vol. 4, p. 444). For *Roderick*, Scott expressed sincere admiration, but he also felt that Southey's life was too secluded and that he was surrounded by a too admiring circle of family and friends.

Two events could have hindered the friendship. Southey's connection with the *Edinburgh Annual Register* ultimately involved him in the loss of expected income – indeed he ceased to contribute after the fourth volume because he was not paid. The evidence is not clear, but Southey presumably received several years later part of what was owing him through Scott's intervention since Scott had assured him 'no exertion of any influence I can use with them shall be wanting if necessary.' The appointment of Scott's son-in-law, John G. Lockhart, brought a change in Southey's relations with the *Quarterly*, but Scott, who had had no part in the business of the appointment, was able to mollify Southey and also ensure his continuance as a contributor – although on a less frequent scale – to the *Quarterly*.

A final quotation from Scott's *Journal* is eloquent and touching. In the midst of Scott's financial troubles and bankruptcy in 1826 he recorded in his journal: 'He [Lockhart] mentions poor Southey testifying much interest for me even to tears. It is odd – Am I so hard-hearted a man? I could not have wept for him though in distress I would have gone any length to serve him' (*Journal*, p. 160).

Southey first met Charles Lamb in January, 1795 when he went from Bristol to London in quest of Coleridge. Lamb was then only a month shy of his twentieth birthday. Lamb became an ardent admirer of Southey's poems, both long and short, and his letters contain many a complimentary phrase and sentence about these early works. Lamb's friendship with Southey flourished during Southey's various residences in London between 1797 and 1802. During 1798, on Southey's absences from the city, Lamb made Southey his chief correspondent (Lamb did not keep the letters he received so that we have only his side of the correspondence). Lamb contributed to the *Annual Anthology* along with his friends the Tobins. The meetings in later years after Southey's removal to Keswick were of necessity few in number, but occasional letters were exchanged, and Lamb was urged to visit the Lake District. In 1823 a contretemps occurred through, ironically enough, a wish of Southey to do his old friend a service by a favorable mention of the recently published *Essays of Elia*, but the phrase in his review: 'Elia's Essays, a book which wants only a sounder religious feeling, to be as delightful as it is original' was not revised because the proofs never came. Southey's explanation was:

I had written that it wanted nothing to render it altogether delightful but a *saner* religious feeling. *This* would have been the proper word if any other person had written the book. Feeling its extreme unfitness as soon as it was written, I altered it

immediately for the first word which came into my head,
intending to re-model the sentence when it should come to me
in the proof; and that proof never came.

Lamb, offended, printed a public letter to Southey in the *London
Magazine*, but Southey refused to engage in any quarrel over an
unintended slight and unfortunate phrase: '. . . . no infirmity of mind
on his part shall make me act or feel unkindly towards one whose
sterling goodness I respect as much as I admire his genius' (Bowles,
p. 37). Southey's explanatory letter brought an immediate answer
from Lamb and a suggestion of a personal meeting at the next opportunity. Lamb's words included 'I have been fighting against a
shadow. . . . My guardian angel was absent at that time.' In 1830
Southey was able to make a public *amende* to Lamb by coming to his
defence after William Jerdan's strong attack upon Lamb's *Album
Verses*. Southey's poem entitled 'To Charles Lamb, On the Reviewal
of his *Album Verses* in the *Literary Gazette*,' was published in *The Times*
of August 6, 1830. Not many years remained for Lamb, who died in
January, 1834. On hearing of the news, Southey commented: 'Never
was there a kinder, a more generous, or a more feeling heart than his'
(*Letters*, vol. 4, p. 394).

Southey's friendship with Landor is a satisfactory relationship to
record since it was never marred by any quarrel or misunderstanding
nor by any change in the mutual esteem each felt for the other. The
quarrelsome and litigious side of Landor's temperament never appeared.
Southey had been an admirer of Landor's anonymously published
Gebir (1798), and their first meeting in 1808 was an unqualified success.
From this occasion Southey received the stimulus to resume the composition of *Kehama*, the publication of which Landor had generously
offered to finance. Although their meetings were few, the two men of
letters remained in communication throughout Southey's life, and
after Southey's death Landor proved a faithful friend to the widow
and the son Cuthbert. In August, 1811 Southey was a guest for two or
three days at Landor's Welsh estate of Llanthony, and during the
summer of 1817 Southey spent three days with Landor at Como in
Italy. In 1832 Landor paid a visit to the Lake District and visited
Southey at Greta Hall. Their last meeting occurred during November
1836 on Southey's final visit to his native city of Bristol. Southey's
personal influence over Landor was great, and he was able to persuade
him to eliminate passages from the *Imaginary Conversations* that could

have resulted in suits of libel. 'I struck out passages with a freedom which was taken by Landor as it was meant' (*New Letters*, vol. 2, p. 326). Since Landor was hypersensitive in all that pertained to himself as author this is indeed a tribute to the depth of the friendship and the respect Landor felt for Southey's judgment. A dozen years earlier Southey recommended that Landor's *Charles James Fox: A Commentary on his Life and Character*, an answer to B. J. Trotter's memoirs of Fox, should not be published. Landor's rashness would certainly involve its author in litigation. The work, although actually printed, was suppressed and not published until 1907. Southey, for his part, praised Landor's work in print, his review of Landor's *Count Julian* appearing in the *Quarterly* during 1812. The benefits of this friendship were shared by each, Southey deriving much from the esteem and encouragement of a fellow-poet. Landor almost venerated Southey. 'Virtue, wisdom, and genius, he united in a higher degree, and more interfused, than any other creature I have known. His friendship is the main glory of my life' (*Fragmentary Remains . . . of Sir Humphry Davy*, 1858, p. 50). Landor introduced Southey into four of his dialogues: two between Southey and Porson, and two between Southey and Landor himself. Landor was ever jealous of Southey's reputation, talked – perhaps at too great length on occasion – about Southey's greatness, and after Southey's death wrote tributes to his memory.

The Byron-Southey relationship is the most prominent of all Southey had with his literary contemporaries, and save for one or two personal meetings, was conducted in the press, in poems, and in appendices to various books, aided and abetted – we are led to believe from references in memoirs and letters of the Byron circle – by rumor and gossip. Byron first paid his respects to Southey in 1809, in *English Bards and Scotch Reviewers*, in witty couplets in a time-honored satiric tradition. In 1813, at the time of Southey's appointment to the laureateship, Southey and Byron met at Holland House, where Southey was a guest of Lord Holland. Southey reported that in Byron 'I saw a man whom in voice, manner and countenance I liked very much more than either his character or his writings had given me reason to expect.' Byron was impressed by Southey's good looks and quipped to Tom Moore 'the best-looking bard I have seen for some time. To have that poet's head and shoulders, I would almost have written his Sapphics.' In his Journal he recorded a very high estimate: 'His appearance is *Epic*; and he is the only existing entire man of letters. All the others have some pursuit annexed to their authorship. His manners are mild, but not those of a man of the world, and his talents of the first order. His prose is perfect. Of his poetry there are various opinions: there is, perhaps, too much of it for the present generation; posterity will probably select. He has *passages* equal to anything' (Byron, *Letters and Journals*, vol. 2, pp. 266, 331). Byron later admired *Roderick* (1814) as 'near perfection as poetry can be – which considering how I dislike that school I wonder at.' Byron, after leaving England, became increasingly sensitive to criticism of himself and his circle. He attributed the remarks in the *Quarterly Review* of Hunt's *Foliage* on Shelley to Southey (the article was probably by J. T. Coleridge). He had also heard a rumor – from what source is unclear – that Southey had described him and Shelley as 'in a league of incest' together, a rumor Southey later denied. The attacks on Southey in the first cantos of *Don Juan* were written against this background, but although the dedicatory lines were not published in 1819, Southey had heard of them. The preface to Southey's *Vision of Judgment* (1821) was his answer to this attack and to others from this school describing the school of younger poets – Hunt, Shelley, and Byron with perhaps Tom Moore – as the Satanic school. Byron replied in Canto II of *Don Juan* and in the prose appendix to *The Two Foscari*. Southey answered the latter in a letter to the *Courier* (reprinted in *Life*, vol. 6, and his *Essays*, 1832). This letter so enraged Byron that, according to Medwin, 'his colour changed almost prismatically; his lips were as pale as death.' Southey's preface and poem, written in an attempt to adapt hexameters in English, a feat no one has successfully performed, invited a reply. Byron's reply was devastating, and has for the bulk of readers of English poetry fixed their view of Southey. Southey did not respond, and his correspondence has almost no reference to Byron's poem. A final letter to the *Courier* (December 7, 1824) answered certain charges in Medwin's *Conversations* to the effect that he was not the author of the review of *Foliage* and complaining that many papers in that review were falsely ascribed to him. A contemporary reviewer in *Blackwood's* commented in a non-partisan fashion:

> Mr. Southey is, and always was, too much of a monk, to understand a man of the world like Byron; and Byron was too decidedly, rather too exclusively a man of the world to understand a monk like Southey. Hence this absurd exaggeration of each other's errors and defects. In Southey, one of the most learned and accomplished scholars, and pure and virtuous men . . .

Byron could see nothing but the Tory partizan. . . . In Byron, on the other hand, in one of the greatest of the great Poets of England . . . Southey could see nothing else but a 'pander-general to youthful vice,' and the founder of 'a Satanic school' (*Blackwood's*, vol. 16, p. 711).

Unfortunately, the quarrel does not place either poet in a favorable light – oversensitivity, a certain degree of self-righteousness, a willingness to believe unfounded gossip, and a too great willingness to air private grievance and pique in public. For Byron and his reputation the contretemps may have helped simply because it provided – what could not have been foreseen – the occasion for his brilliant satire, *The Vision of Judgment*. But for Southey's reputation it was not only unfortunate but perhaps disastrous. For it must be that poem that determines the attitude of the average reader of poetry – be he amateur or professional student.

Southey's connection with Shelley has already been described earlier in this study, but two poets, elevated today to the first rank, deserve mention. William Blake, known to very few of his contemporary poets, met Southey through Henry Crabb Robinson on July 24, 1811: 'Southey,' Robinson records in his diary, 'had been with Blake, and admired both his designs and his poetic talents, at the same time that he held him for a decided madman. Blake, he says, spoke of his visions with the diffidence that is usual with such people, and did not seem to expect that he should be believed. He showed Southey a perfectly mad poem called *Jerusalem* – Oxford Street is in Jerusalem' (*Henry Crabb Robinson on Books and Their Writers*, 1938, vol. 1, pp. 40–41). But the visit made an impression on Southey and years later he mentioned Blake and quoted his poem 'The Flea' in *The Doctor*.

John Keats's connection with Southey is slight, but Keats had read – and was perhaps influenced by – several of Southey's poems, and Southey was familiar enough to comment on January 30, 1821 to the young poet, John Heraud, that 'Keats buries himself in the exuberance of his ornaments' (Edith Heraud, *Memoirs of John A. Heraud*, 1898, p. 26). Southey had objected several times about the acrimonious criticism of poetry in the *Quarterly* in letters to Murray, and commented to Scott in 1824 of 'that injustice and cruelty (for example) which was shown towards Keats' in the notorious review of *Endymion* (*New Letters*, vol. 2, p. 268).

Part II

Prose

Introduction

Although Southey began his literary career as a poet with a collaborative volume of *Poems* (1795) with Robert Lovell, and *Joan of Arc* (1796), he turned very early to prose partly because, as a writer dependent upon his pen for his livelihood, there was a ready market from publishers for whatever he wrote. His first work in prose was a travel book based upon his travels in Spain and Portugal in 1795–96, *Letters Written During a Short Residence in Spain and Portugal* (1797), and in the same year he found that the editors of the *Monthly Magazine* and the *Critical Review* would pay him for reviews and miscellaneous contributions. Much of this writing he regarded as task work, and he always looked forward to the day when he could afford to give up reviewing, but that day never came, and he continued to do an occasional review-article to the very last year of his working life.

Southey's prose falls into several classifications, although the categories overlap to some degree. His most praised and most important category is that of biography and autobiography: his *Life of Nelson*, his letters, his journals, and *The Doctor*, that curious mixture of fiction and autobiography. The second category in importance is that of social and political criticism of which his *Letters from England by Don Manuel Alvarez Espriella* and his *Colloquies on the Progress and Prospects of Society* stand out. In sheer bulk Southey's histories loom large, especially his *History of the Peninsular War* and his *History of Brazil*. His *Book of the Church*, designed as a popular history of the Church of England, is the one historical work combining secular with religious history, which has many chapters of interest for the reader today. Lesser categories of importance are Southey's reviews, for the most part still buried within the files of the *Annual Review* and the *Quarterly Review*, and his various translations and editions of such

Spanish-Portuguese works as *Amadis of Gaul, Palmerin of England,* and the *Cid,* and his editions and biographies of Bunyan and Cowper.

The achievement is impressive, so recognized in its day, and if not many of these books are read today, they reflect the interests of the age as well as the interests and personality of the author who wrote them. They are still worthy of description and comment, and not a few can still be read with pleasure and profit.

3

Social and Political Criticism

Much of the best and most interesting comment about Southey's prose has been focused upon his writings on social and political questions, and this category can well serve as the most convenient introduction to a study of his prose. These comments about his social and political writings are about equally divided between censure and praise. Southey received during his literary lifetime a constant barrage of abuse from those who espoused a different political philosophy, so that he is usually thought of as a writer who supported the *status quo* for venal reasons not unconnected with his writing for the *Quarterly Review*, which supported the ministerial party, and later with his appointment as Poet Laureate.

But to attempt to read Southey's social and political writing as the expression of a writer devoted to the political positions of the ministerial party – an administration which literary historians usually call a Tory administration – is to do Southey a disservice and to misunderstand the various political groups which headed the British government during his lifetime. The changing conditions of the domestic and foreign scene – changes that no one could have foreseen – meant that individuals and government were necessarily shifting their sympathies. Southey was not a systematic political theorist, but he held certain views throughout his life and altered others as he grew older and feared some of the changes he saw coming. A constant thread throughout his career was a concern for humanity, a hatred for cruelty and injustice, and a sympathy for the poor and outcasts. Thus came his early advocacy of the abolition of slavery and the slave trade, his opposition to cruel and unreasonable punishments incorporated into military and civil law, and his distress over the exploitation of the laboring poor and especially children working in factories. These humanitarian concerns led to his writing in favor of reforms in prisons and in the care of the mentally ill and towards the efforts of the Quakers who led in these two reforms.

Southey's early enthusiasm for the French Revolution was cooled by the turn of events in France, and he came to look upon Napoleon as the enemy of British freedom and security and a foe who must be defeated at all costs. From this belief came his support of the ministers who were directing the war and his willingness to write in aid of these policies in the *Edinburgh Annual Register* and the *Quarterly Review*, founded as they were to support the ministry against the pacifism and defeatism of some of the Whigs. Southey also supported the ministers in their opposition to any concessions to the Roman Catholics and to reforms in the process by which Members of Parliament were elected. But many of the reforms which he did recommend were viewed by the most conservative, whether Whig or Tory, as subversive of the constitution.

The use of the word 'Tory' – a label usually given to describe Southey – has a complex history. The word is seldom used during the early nineteenth century except in an historical sense as it was used during the late seventeenth century. Denis Grey, the biographer of Spencer Perceval (1762–1812), states that Perceval never used the word, and yet Perceval has been considered the most Tory of Tory ministers. I am not aware that Southey ever uses the word Tory to describe himself, and the word, in fact, seldom appears in his writing. The only citations for 'Tory' from the early nineteenth century in the *New English Dictionary* are historical references to the seventeenth century and not to contemporary political parties. Although Southey mentions the Whigs, he normally refers to political groups by such phrases as Pittites, Foxites, Grenvillites, the ins and outs, and he coined a phrase 'the Gregres' to describe the coalition between the followers of Lord Grenville and of Lord Grey. The explanation for this usage is the rather simple one that political parties lacked the strong party discipline they later achieved. Parliament consisted of rather loosely attached groups as well as of many members who thought of themselves as independent country gentlemen. Indeed, the group of ministers in power at any given time often had great difficulty in gaining support for important crucial issues. It is, therefore, somewhat misleading to give Southey the label of 'Tory' when the word had such a vague and uncertain denotation during his lifetime – whatever may have become its meaning and connotation later in the nineteenth and twentieth centuries.

Letters from England by Don Manuel Alvarez Espriella

Southey's views on political and social problems are agreeably set forth in various passages of his *Letters from England by Don Manuel Alvarez Espriella*, a series of letters supposedly written by a young Spaniard resident in England for a year and a half. Published in 1807 when Southey was thirty-two, the Espriella letters present his views on a variety of subjects and contain most of the ideas and points of view which he later expanded in his reviews for the *Quarterly* and in his *Colloquies on the Progress and Prospects of Society* (1829).

The chronological arrangement of the letters – Don Manuel was supposedly in England from April, 1802 until October, 1803 – does not provide a systematic account of these social and political events, so that the reader must skip around. Letter 12 in praise of the ministry of Addington – who displaced Pitt in March, 1801 – shows Southey's deep distrust for Pitt's ministry and its repressive measures. With Addington all was changed: 'The system of terror, of alarm, and of espionage has been laid aside, the most burthensome of the taxes repealed.' Southey's support of later ministries came only after Pitt's death in 1806, and Spencer Perceval was the first Prime Minister to receive Southey's whole-hearted support because of that ministry's commitment to the Spanish cause in the Peninsular War. Don Manuel found many aspects of English law praiseworthy such as the prohibition of torture and unusual punishments, but reforms were needed. In Letter 22 the harshness of the law providing for the death penalty for forgery is censured, the famous case of Dr William Dodd and Dr Johnson's efforts on his behalf being told as an example. 'More persons,' Don Manuel comments, 'have suffered for this offence since the law has been enacted than for any other crimes' (ed. J. Simmons, 1951, p. 123 – all page references to Espriella are to this edition).

Although Southey later considered Sir Francis Burdett a dangerous radical, Letter 48 shows the author taking the side of Burdett against Pitt when in 1797 Burdett questioned the treatment of prisoners when the habeas corpus act was suspended. 'But pride and obstinacy are the predominant parts of Mr Pitt's character; right or wrong he never yields; and he now chose to show his power by protecting the gaoler in defiance of public opinion' (p. 281). Reforms were likewise needed in the army where the cruel practice of flogging (Letter 10) was still

77

practiced, and the need for a limited service bill was stressed, but bills
to effect these changes were repeatedly voted down. This same letter
proposed a system of public works after the Roman system for dis-
charged soldiers: road building, canal digging, cultivation of waste
lands, together with villages for the housing of the soldiers' families.
In addition, Don Manuel thought all boys should be trained in the
use of arms.

ł As Don Manuel traveled through England he had opportunity to
see the effect in human terms of the consequences of English trade and
manufacture, and what he saw horrified him. Southey was one of the
first to cry out at the terrible price being paid in terms of human
misery, exploitation of children, and environmental pollution for the
great rise in national wealth and value of exports. In his description of
Birmingham and Manchester he anticipated the twentieth-century
concern for the loss of fresh air and the damage and destruction to
plant life in the description of the environs of Birmingham:

> A heavy cloud of smoke hung over the city, above which in
> many places black columns were sent up with prodigious force
> from the steam-engines . . . the tower of some manufactory was
> to be seen in the distance, vomiting up flames and smoke, and
> blasting every thing around with its metallic vapours. . . .
> Instead of cottages we saw streets of brick hovels, blackened with
> the smoke of coal fires which burn day and night in these dismal
> regions (p. 203).

He was appalled by the sight of small children tending the machinery:
'I thought that if Dante had peopled one of his hells with children,
here was a scene worthy to have supplied him with new images of
torment' (p. 208). His final judgment was:

> In no other country can such riches be acquired by commerce,
> but it is the one who grows rich by the labour of the hundred. . . .
> They are deprived in childhood of all instruction and all
> enjoyment; of the sports in which childhood instinctively
> indulges, of fresh air by day and of natural sleep by night.
> Their health physical and moral is alike destroyed; they die of
> diseases induced by unremitting task work, by confinement in
> the impure atmosphere of crowded rooms, by the particles of
> metallic or vegetable dust which they are continually inhaling;
> or they live to grow up without decency, without comfort, and

without hope, without morals, without religion, and without shame, and bring forth slaves like themselves to tread in the same path of misery (pp. 209–10).

Many details in the Espriella letters recapture the style of living in a comfortable English home such as the one in which Don Manuel was a guest. We learn, for instance, in Letter 15 of the furnishings of a house – the carpets on the floor, the fire-place and its mantel, the bell ropes, the chairs and tables of the fashionable mahogany (often veneered), and even of the kitchen range designed after Count Rumford's plans. In comparison to the furnishings of a Spanish house the English house contained many luxuries – even superfluities. The following passages describe everyday customs: Letter 15, the English breakfast; Letter 13, the clothes and shops and scenes in London streets; and Letter 17, great detail concerning household gadgets such as knives and toasting forks. Francis Jeffrey in his review of Espriella in the *Edinburgh* objected to all these details, but they make Espriella a valuable source for life in 1807. Most writers neglect to mention the minutiae of daily living so that subsequent generations have difficulty in reconstructing the background of life in a past era.

The character or persona of Don Manuel is an appealing one. A young man writing letters home to members of his family and to his Father Confessor, he remembers the affectionate ties with his family in Spain and is appreciative of the kind attention and courtesies extended to him by his new English friends in whose household he was living. He is an acute observer of all sights and sounds from the moment of his arrival at Falmouth until his departure a year and a half later from that same port. The portrait of Don Manuel was so convincing that some readers accepted the book as a genuine report of a Spanish traveler. Anna Seward, however, suspected it for what it was because of the skill of the writing and the smoothness of the translation. It was too good to be from the pen of the impressionable young Spaniard! Actually, Southey in his depiction of Don Manuel is often writing his own description: Southey himself – an indefatigable writer of letters – who had an eye for picturesque detail in landscape and in human character. Don Manuel is essentially a kind, affectionate, and decent young man who appreciates hospitality and the offer of friendly services.

The greatest flaw in *Letters from England* to a reader of the present day is the excessive number of letters devoted to religious groups. The

Quakers, the Jews, Richard Brothers, Joanna Southcott, Swedenborgianism, the Methodists – each receives a separate letter, and to these must be added accounts of churches and cathedrals, where curious bits of ecclesiastical history or biography are often interpolated. The proportion of space devoted to this aspect of English life seems out of balance: indeed Letter 29 on the number of the sects and something of their history would inform the reader of today of all that he might wish to know.

The Espriella letters are not wanting in humor; indeed there is an undercurrent present in most of the descriptions of English customs. Southey's experiences in Spain and Portugal gave him just enough knowledge of the contrasts between the countries to give Don Manuel's expressions of incredulity, disgust, or astonishment an aura of verisimilitude. Making fun of the ways of the Englishman has always been a source of amusement to the English reader. The last paragraph of Letter 16 on the paradoxical English combines humor with insight into the English character:

This spirit of contradiction is the character of the nation. They love to be at war, but do not love to pay for their amusement; and now, that they are at peace, they begin to complain that the newspapers are not worth reading, and rail at the French as if they really wished to begin again. There is not a people upon the earth who have a truer love for their Royal family than the English, yet they caricature them in the most open and insolent manner. They boast of the freedom of the press, yet as surely and systematically punish the author who publishes anything obnoxious, and the bookseller who sells it, as we in our country should prevent the publication. They cry out against intolerance, and burn down the houses of those whom they regard as heretics. They love liberty; go to war with their neighbours, because they chose to become republicans, and insist upon the right of enslaving the negroes. They hate the French and ape all their fashions, ridicule their neologisms and then naturalize them, laugh at their inventions and then adopt them, cry out against their political measures and then imitate them; the levy in mass, the telegraph, and the income-tax are all from France. And the common people, not to be behind-hand with their betters in absurdity, boast as heartily of the roast beef of Old England, as if they were not obliged to be content themselves with bread and

potatoes. Well may punch be the favourite liquor of the
English, – it is a truly emblematic compound of contrarieties
(pp. 92–93).

Another humorous passage is the satirical picture of the English who,
moving from a comfortable home to uncomfortable lodgings, annually
proceed to fashionable watering places, often for the purpose of seeking
marriages for their eligible daughters:

> These people . . . crowd themselves into the narrow apartments
> and dark streets of a little country town. . . . The price they pay
> for these lodgings is exorbitant; the more expensive the place,
> the more numerous are the visitors. . . . They go into the country
> for the sake of seeing company, not for retirement; and in all
> this there is more reason than you perhaps have yet imagined. . . .
> They who have daughters take them to these public places to
> look for husbands; and there is no indelicacy in this, because
> others who have no such motive for frequenting them go
> likewise, in consequence of the fashion, or of the habits which
> they have acquired in their younger days (pp. 164–5, Letter 30).

What are the best things in the Espriella letters? The answer must
be those letters descriptive of journeys and the cities and places visited.
Mixed with anecdotes of incidents of travel, travelling by stagecoach,
stops at inns, chance encounters with other travellers, the letters contain
perceptive accounts of many famous spots such as York Minster and
other great cathedrals. The *Edinburgh Review* especially commended
the description of the Lake District (Letters 41–4), and that judgment
seems sound. Southey had been resident for three to four years at
Keswick and had come to love the beauties of the region and had
walked over most of the places Don Manuel describes:

> Everything grows upon me. I become daily more and more
> sensible of the height of the mountains, observe their forms with
> a more discriminating eye, and watch with increased pleasure the
> wonderful changes they assume under the effects of clouds or
> sunshine (p. 237).

Here the voice is that of Southey recounting his own growing affection
for the land that was to be his home for the rest of his life. In any
anthology of descriptions of the Lake District these chapters in
Espriella deserve an honored place.

The social historian has found in the Espriella letters an excellent picture of life in England during the years 1802–6, and the work has been expertly read and quoted by several writers, notably Arthur Bryant in his *Years of Endurance* (1942), pp. 24, 174, 337, 357, and in *Years of Victory* (1944), pp. 17, 19.

Colloquies on the Progress and Prospects of Society

Southey's *Colloquies on the Progress and Prospects of Society* (1829) has enjoyed among all his later works the widest popularity and recognition, especially from historians interested in tracing ideas and movements in the nineteenth century. In addition however, the work has considerable literary merit and a carefully contrived setting. The book opens with a description of the author in his study at twilight in a half-dreaming, half-waking state. This reverie is interrupted by a visitor, who is none other than the ghost of Sir Thomas More, who introduces himself with a discussion of ghosts. The author, who gives himself the name of Montesinos, encounters this ghostly visitor on several occasions, and each visit develops into a discussion of some topic of current interest. These visits afford Southey the opportunity to describe several picturesque spots in the Lake District, since his ghostly visitor appears not only at night but also in broad daylight. This setting provides for an alteration of these scenes of description with abstract discussion. The first edition of the *Colloquies* is furthermore illustrated with six engravings after drawings by William Westall of the spots described in the book and by a frontispiece of More's portrait by Holbein.

Southey's *Colloquies* affords a reader a chance to learn anew of his positions on most of the topics he had discussed in the *Quarterly Review*, the *Annual Review*, and in his Espriella letters. Montesinos and More discuss a variety of controversial topics, with many glances at historical sources and parallels. These topics were the problems of poverty, the manufacturing system, emancipation of Roman Catholics, national education, emigration, the position of women in modern society, the growth of infidelity, the spread of subversive and revolutionary ideas by the printing press that threatened revolution, and the means that could be taken to deal with these problems. Southey pleaded for a more humane administration of the poor laws and for a system of national education which would provide for religious education on some such scheme as Dr Andrew Bell's Madras system whereby one master by using the abilities of the older students to teach the less advanced could teach several hundred. These national schools would be under the guidance of the Church. Southey also saw the need for new universities and recommended that a new one be established at Durham. He recommended that the government take direct action to regulate such problems as child labor in the factories, the pollution of the environment in the large manufacturing cities, and the uncontrolled construction of houses in the new towns. Southey's voice was one of the first to cry out against the insanitary conditions of life in these cities and to complain of the ugly and depressing surroundings in which the new generation was growing up. He was aware that many thousands of persons were helpless in the face of the new conditions of labor when because of improved technology or the working of economic cycles large groups of people were suddenly without either employment or the means of subsistence. If Southey's grasp of the economic and monetary causes of these problems was not always professionally acute, his feeling was right. Aware of the large numbers of persons who had difficulty in earning a livelihood – even in the educated middle classes – he recommended emigration to the British colonies or to the United States as a way out. He was also dimly aware of the future power of a British commonwealth of nations based upon new and powerful nations overseas that would be linked to Britain by the ties of language, law, and a common cultural heritage. The government should take steps to assist these persons to establish themselves in their new homes and not simply let them fend for themselves when they reached the remote areas of Canada or Australia. The government should also undertake a vast system of public works which would not only provide useful employment for the unemployed but would provide needed improvements such as the reclamation of waste lands, the building of roads and footpaths, new schools, colleges, and should make allotments of arable lands to disbanded service men and other unemployed. As a further means of giving support to self-respecting working men he recommended the formation of savings banks. Reform of the laws could also be invoked to improve society. Repeal of the game laws would mean that the poor would no longer be tempted to poach and steal game. If Southey thought that the government should not let the people starve, so should they not be starved for want of knowledge, both secular and religious. Education and religion were indeed inseparable, and the two would enrich the lives of the people as human beings.

Throughout the *Colloquies* Southey stressed the higher value of the spiritual and moral aspects of life to the material. As a corollary to this belief he emphasized the responsibility of the state to provide religious education for the masses and he asserted that 'It is not more directly the duty of a government to provide for the defence and safety of the commonwealth, than it is to provide religious instruction for the people' (vol. 2, p. 46). The government had neglected to provide churches in those areas where the population had been growing, and it had failed also in providing proper stipends for clergy in places of small population where the parishioners were likewise poor. But the results of this neglect were appalling with thousands of persons crowded into the new manufacturing centers ignorant of any religion. 'These people are unbelievers . . . because, as far as regards all moral culture, all needful instruction, all humanizing and redeeming influences, they are left like savages, in the very midst of cultivated society' (vol. 2, p. 105). Fortunately, the Methodists had done something to repair these deficiencies. But with all that needed to be done, the Church was in danger of losing what wealth it had, and Southey saw in the dissenters, Methodists and Roman Catholics, groups who were eager to bring about this spoliation of church property. To repeal the Test Acts which applied to dissenters and to admit Roman Catholics into Parliament would only be hastening that day. Southey's measures for countering these problems were to encourage through scholarships more youths to enter the Church – some of whom might otherwise become dissenting and Methodist ministers – to found a new University, perhaps at Durham, in some way to encourage learning at the University – where at present it languished – and to provide national education upon Dr Bell's system. Southey's position is summed up in More's words: 'To maintain that the state ought not to concern itself with the religion of the subjects is the greatest and most perilous of all political errors: and to regard religion with indifference is the most dangerous of all moral ones' (vol. 1, p. 133).

The faults of the *Colloquies* are many. Southey wrote too often from a lack of first-hand knowledge. This deficiency is very apparent in his treatment of Spanish America and of the United States where his comments, although not unsympathetic, were the result of his reading among historians and travellers. Discussions of economics and monetary theory are at best difficult for the layman or journalist, and Southey's lack of knowledge is evident, but his comments have value because of his focus upon the human consequences of these impersonal economic forces. His own values are much to the forefront of whatever he is discussing. His own predilection for a life of quiet study in a pleasant rural environment, for instance, can be traced in his regret at the passing of so much that was aesthetically attractive in the countryside. He also regretted the loss of old customs and the dispersion of so many persons from the places where they and their ancestors had been rooted for generations. There was for him a great value for the individual and family who had local and hereditary attachments to a particular place extending for many generations.

Economic issues are prominent in many of the discussions between More and Montesinos. Southey views with mixed feelings the growth of national wealth when this growth is accompanied by the financial losses of small shopkeepers and small farmers who are crowded out by larger and more efficient economic units. 'National wealth is wholesome only when it is equitably diffused' (vol. 2, p. 253). As economic necessity forced young people to leave their homes and seek their fortunes in commercial centers, to Canada, the United States, or Australia: 'There is evil, great evil, in this disruption of natural ties . . . this weakening of the domestic affections . . . this premature dissolution of them.' But he observed that every walk of life was crowded – in the crafts, in trade, in the army and navy, in the courts of law, and in medicine. But Southey had faith in the willingness of the poor to work, and it was the duty of the government to provide opportunities. With so many waste lands in the country many could be employed in making them productive, and those who could not be accommodated at home could be encouraged to establish themselves in the colonies. Although Southey seemed to emphasize the losses which society suffered by the changes, he did not deny the benefits that the new manufacturing system had brought: it had enabled England to defeat Napoleon and to produce ships and specie.

The position of Southey towards the Roman Catholics is the one that is most likely to irritate and alienate the reader of the present day. The position, however, can be understood – if not accepted – by considering his own experiences and the attitude of most Englishmen of his day, whether aristocrats, middle class, or city mob. The Protestant ascendancy was a part of the Constitution and the king's coronation oath required him to maintain the Protestant religion, and the law further provided for the Protestant succession. The Catholic question was deeply involved with the Irish question, and the average Englishman thought of the Irish as barbaric and disloyal. Any opening, no matter how small, that would make it possible for Catholics to participate and in time to dominate the political structure should be resisted lest unimaginable terrors be loosed in the land. Southey, with his firsthand experience of Portugal and Spain where the Roman Church was ascendant, had been shocked by what he saw of a priest-dominated society. The memory of the Inquisition was still fresh there and stories were still current of *autos-da-fé*. In France the Roman Church was associated with the despotism of the Bourbons and in Italy with Papal tyranny and misrule. Southey and those who knew their British history remembered the burnings at Smithfield, the martyrdom of Latimer, Ridley, and Cranmer, and the Glorious Revolution of 1688. The fact that the worst fears of those who opposed Catholic Emancipation were not realized does not deny the reality of those fears. There is always some risk in changing a system that has given the country a long period of stable government. As the historian John Derry observes in this connection: '. . . men who thought that the established Constitution in Church and State was the greatest bulwark of order in an increasingly unstable world were not entirely unjustified in claiming that to tamper with the Old Order in one respect was to expose it to more far-reaching attacks' (*Reaction and Reform*, 1963, pp. 96–7). Southey and others were correct in gauging the political and disruptive forces that can be loosed when political and economic problems are exacerbated by religious emotions, and certainly the violent disturbances in Ireland, the recent Arab-Israeli war, and the conflict betwen Pakistan and India provide present proof of the destructive power of religious differences. Southey, however, was not correct in his assessment of the situation and its possible dangers in 1829.

A few other topics from the *Colloquies* deserve mention. Southey's discussion of the position of women in society is a far cry from twentieth-century discussions of this problem, but Southey was concerned over the limited opportunities open to women obliged to earn their own livelihood, the social prejudices against those in trade, and the actual distress and poverty to which many women of the middle class were reduced when financial reverses came to their families or when the death of a father and husband removed their means of support. Southey had long regretted the loss which England and the Church of England had suffered by the suppression of the monasteries in the sixteenth century, and he had been favorably impressed by the example of the Beguines in Belgium. 'Why then have you no Beguines, no Sisters of Charity,' he asks:

Why in the most needful, the most merciful form that charity can take, have you not followed the example of the French and the Netherlanders? No Vincent de Paul has been heard in your pulpits; no Louise le Gras has appeared among the daughters of Great Britain! Piety has not found its way into your prisons; your hospitals are imploring it in vain; nothing is wanting in them but religious charity, and oh what a want is that! (vol. 2, p. 318).

Looking forward, Southey hoped that within thirty years England would have such houses as the Beguines since there was about them 'nothing Romish, nothing superstitious' but only 'what is righteous and holy.' Sixteen years after the publication of the *Colloquies*, the first religious order for women was established. William E. Gladstone, who composed the circular issued by the promoters of this first sisterhood, began with a quotation from the *Colloquies*. Lord John Manners, an admirer of Southey and a leader in the Young England movement, recorded that when in 1843 a memorial was considered in honor of Southey he had recommended the establishment of a Sisterhood of Mercy (P. F. Anson, *The Call of the Cloister*, London, 1956, pp. 226–7). Although Southey would have found much in the Anglo-Catholic movement to which he could not subscribe, the leaders of that group found in Southey's writings and especially in the *Colloquies* much to encourage them.

Two other matters deserve brief mention. The sympathetic portrayal of Sir Thomas More, one of Southey's heroes from the past, is of literary interest and contributes to the charm of the book. More is not presented so much as the adversary, or devil's advocate, for Montesinos, but rather as another aspect of the same author. Southey shows himself learned in details of More's life and writings and, if not always approving of all of More's actions in his life, making the point that every man must be judged by the circumstances of his own times. The last Colloquy of the *Colloquies* is devoted to Southey's library and is largely a description of it and the associations of many of the books that it contained. The reader who wishes to know Southey in many of his most attractive aspects should direct his attention to his *Colloquies*.

The *Colloquies* may be best known to some readers because of T. B. Macaulay's review of the work in the *Edinburgh Review*. The reading of this review can be recommended as corrective of the commonly held view that Southey is 'reactionary' and Macaulay and the Whigs 'progressive.' The exact opposite is rather the case. Macaulay, after reviewing in both laudatory and depreciatory phrases Southey's literary career, proceeds to answer the charges that Southey brings upon contemporary society. Macaulay views the manufacturing system as having brought great benefits to society and having greatly reduced the numbers of persons dependent upon poor relief. Macaulay has only contempt for Southey's picture of pleasant rural cottages in contrast to the aesthetically displeasing houses of the workers in manufacturing towns and dismisses Southey's position with these words:

> Rose-bushes and poor rates, rather than steam-engines and
> independence. Mortality and cottages with weather-stains, rather
> than health and long life with edifices which time cannot mellow.

Southey's recommendation that public works be undertaken whereby to improve society is countered by Macaulay's statement that after state buildings have been erected such construction should stop. Macaulay deeply distrusted governmental projects such as canals and railroads: 'We firmly believe, that five hundred thousand pounds subscribed by individuals for rail-roads or canals would produce more advantage to the public than five millions voted by Parliament for the same purpose.' Macaulay is likewise opposed to any state interference with religion and suppression of publications for any purpose whatever. He is, furthermore, utterly opposed to Southey's position upon Catholic Emancipation. He closes his essay with several pages of exultation upon the superiority of the present condition of England and its people, the result of the manufacturing system and of the policy of the government not to interfere with any aspect of the lives of individuals. The result of the new manufacturing system has been to lower prices and to bring conveniences and comforts within the reach of the public that those who lived in the age of Sir Thomas More could not have dreamt of! Macaulay's rhetorical conclusion is worthy of quotation:

> Our rulers will best promote the improvement of the people by
> strictly confining themselves to their own legitimate duties – by
> leaving capital to find its most lucrative course, commodities
> their fair price, industry and intelligence their natural reward,
> idleness and folly their natural punishment – by maintaining
> peace, by defending property, by diminishing the price of law,

and by observing strict economy in every department of the state. Let the Government do this – the People will assuredly do the rest.

In the fundamental quarrel between the position of Southey and Macaulay certainly future events would have to divide the judgment as to which position was correct. Southey was certainly right in sensing – however inadequate his mastery of statistics and economics – that the plight of the people required extraordinary measures for their alleviation and that the offence to aesthetics by showing the contrast between life in the country and in the manufacturing towns with all its squalor and pollution of the atmosphere was a problem the country would have to face – it could hardly be left to the initiative of the manufacturers. In his demand for education, for a system of emigration that would assist the emigrants to find their place in their new homeland, for the end to many abuses, his awareness of the situation of women, Southey was on the side of the future and because he was aware of the situation of the distressed individual much more sensitive than Macaulay, despite all the latter's superior knowledge of economics and statistics. Macaulay, however, was right in the light of future events in his insistence that the government should not censor publications – to let seditious writings find their own level – and in the gradual separation of the powers of the State over the Church. Macaulay saw the brave new world of his imagination – the year 1930 – as one in which the material things of the good life (largely realized) would be achieved through a system of *laissez-faire* and the manufacturing system; Southey had fears that the system carried with it the seeds of its own destruction – that these gains would be achieved by the loss of clean air, pure water, the loss of an innocent and simple way of life, a degeneracy in morals, and the influence of the Church upon the lives of the people. These problems the State could and should do something about. Macaulay and Southey each had valuable things to say of the future, but Southey's rose bushes and weather-stained cottages cannot be laughed out of court in a decade that has come to value highly space, clean air, and an aesthetically pleasant and healthful environment.

Edinburgh Annual Register

For four years Southey wrote the 'History of the Year' for the first four volumes of the *Edinburgh Annual Register*. These volumes covered the events of 1808 to 1811 and were published two years later from 1810 to 1813. The collecting of information and the writing of these bulky volumes occupied a great deal of Southey's time and energy during these years and contain his attitudes towards most political and social issues. The reading of old Annual Registers is at best a tedious exercise, and the several hundred pages of each volume (457 for 1808 plus 102 of state papers) present a formidable barrier. Geoffrey Carnall in *Robert Southey and His Age* has made effective use of the *Registers* and has skilfully used their evidence in tracing the growth and expression of Southey's political-social views. Any student who seeks a quarry of unmined information concerning Southey would do well to read – or at least scan – these volumes.

The *Edinburgh Annual Register* was modeled upon the old *Annual Register* that had begun publication in 1758 and the *New Annual Register* (1781–1826), and its presentation of material followed their example. The *Register*, a project of Sir Walter Scott and the Ballantynes, had its beginning in a desire to support the ministry in its prosecution of the Peninsular War and to counteract the Whig opposition expressed in Parliament and in the *Edinburgh Review*. It thus owes its beginning to the same forces and to some of the same persons who founded the *Quarterly Review* for similar purposes. Southey was Scott's choice for the historian of the year, and because of Southey's personal familiarity with Spain and Portugal and his wholehearted support of the Spanish people in their struggle against Napoleon, this choice was a good one given the purposes of the founder and the proprietors. The materials of the 'History of the Year' were divided between Foreign and Domestic affairs, and because of the importance of the war most of these volumes were devoted to a description of military campaigns. The domestic affairs were largely narrated through the debates in Parliament. It was the business of the editor to collect as much material as he could from every source open to him which usually meant newspapers, pamphlets, books, and whatever personal information came his way. Since so much had to be described, the author often chose to let the official document do the telling. But there were still ample opportunities for the writer to comment upon official statements, and parliamentary speeches, and in tracing the fortunes of the important bills introduced.

Southey was later able to use his materials about the war in Spain in *The History of the Peninsular War*, and indeed he thought of some such publishing venture at the time he was writing about the war in the

Register. Although he was able to use much of this section of the *Register* for his *History*, he was not able to re-use so thriftily what he had written upon domestic issues. The modern reader will find what he has to say about humanitarian and governmental reforms of more interest than the accounts of battles long ago. But it was these battles that engaged contemporary interest. Scott, who had sought Southey's services as historian, liked on the whole Southey's treatment of the war. He wrote to J. B. S. Morritt with approval:

> . . . the history is written by Southey and though with some tinge
> of opinions which neither you nor I approve yet there is much
> eloquence and a great deal of what every body must admire.
> The principles respecting France are particularly excellent, the
> general tone of political impartiality gives them great weight
> and to my knowledge they are beginning to *tell* among those
> who would have called them *party clamour* through any medium
> (*Letters of Scott*, vol. 2, p. 382).

Southey's partisanship towards the Spanish effort in the war against France, his opposition to granting concessions to the Roman Catholics, and his similar opposition towards reforming parliamentary elections were issues at that time popularly supported and were cornerstones of ministerial policy which the *Register* was founded to defend. In the area of social as opposed to political reform Southey apparently spoke rather for himself than for a party. Most of the reforms which he vigorously advocated in the *Register* were later passed, but during these years suffered regular defeats in Parliament.

Southey found much to say on behalf of the various legal reforms which Sir Samuel Romilly proposed. This is his comment on Romilly's speech in favor of his bill on privately stealing.

> These proceedings have been thus noticed at length, because it is
> to be hoped that they will lead to changes not less extensive
> than beneficial in the whole system of our criminal laws. A
> society, of which Sir Samuel Romilly is a member, has been
> formed for procuring the abolition of the punishment of death
> in all cases. How far the principle upon which they proceed may
> be examined hereafter, when the subject is introduced into
> parliament. We have lived to see the slave trade abolished, and
> limited service introduced into our army, – measures which have
> cleared the character of England from its two foulest stains. Let

us hope and trust that we shall see also a thorough reformation
of our penal laws (vol. 1, part 1, p. 156).

A concern over the reformation of penal laws was but a short step to
concern over prisons. Several investigations had been made of these
conditions, and Southey's rather remarkable recommendation concerning prisons was:

> Place our prisons under the superintendence of the Quakers, and
> they will be made schools of reform and industry which will do
> honour, not only to our age and country, but even to our nature.
> Invite the Methodists to labour there; – these are the hospitals
> in which such soul-practitioners would indeed be useful! (vol. 2,
> part 1, p. 358).

Generally, it can be stated that the four years during which Southey
wrote the 'History of the Year' the *Register* was always on the side of
humanitarian reform and spoke out on behalf of those in the middle
or lower orders of society who suffered at the hands of those in
authority.

So much of the *Register* had of necessity to be concerned with
recording in orderly fashion the events of the year that it was inevitable
that large parts of the work would be routine records of diplomatic
and parliamentary proceedings. There are still, however, many single
chapters or parts of chapters that contain examples of lively writing.
Events that captured the attention of the public regularly occurred,
and a contemporary historian had a wide field of choice. The following, selected somewhat at random, are chapters that can be recommended as lively examples of narrative art whatever may be their
connection with the important events of the day. From the second
volume (1809) the entire account of the investigation into the affair of
the Duke of York and Mrs Clarke cannot fail to entertain. From the
third volume (1810) Sir Francis Burdett's arrest and transfer to the
Tower (chapter 3), the account of the sailor Jeffrey set ashore on
deserted Sombrero Island by the tyrannous Captain Lake (chapter 4),
the gruesome accounts of slavery (chapter 9), and the narrative of
naval actions at Guadaloupe and St Martins (chapter 7) – all these
accounts the reader of today can enjoy. In the fourth volume (1811)
the account of the complicated intrigue of the court of Naples and the
struggle for the control of Sicily is a skilful example of historical
writing at its best.

4

Biography

In biography and autobiography Southey found his most congenial and successful medium. His first ventures in this genre were in the reviews of journals, diaries, and biographies which he wrote for the *Annual Review*, where his task was to digest the book under review and give it a semblance of order. He found the solution to this problem by presenting a straightforward, chronological, and readable account of the life of the person with quotations from his letters and journals. Good early examples of this method are his brief lives of John Wesley and of Colonel John Hutchinson in the *Annual*. His biographical article of Lord Nelson in the *Quarterly* (1810) led directly to Murray's commission of the Nelson biography, which established his reputation as master of the short biography designed for the general reader, rather than the specialist. All Southey's biographies were about men whom he had not known personally so that he usually writes about them in their public rather than in their private aspects. Thus his biographies differ from those of Boswell and Lockhart, and in writing them he depended very largely upon published sources, although he did – especially for his life and edition of Cowper – seek out unpublished letters and documents in the manner of a twentieth-century scholar. His choice of subjects was generally fortunate: Nelson, Wesley, and Cowper were public and respected figures for whom Southey felt a personal sympathy and admiration.

The Life of Nelson

Southey's *Life of Nelson*, his most successful and most popular biography, was also his first. Horatio, Lord Nelson, the national hero and the victor at the battle of Trafalgar, was the single figure of the struggle against Napoleon to capture, by the force of his character and personality, the hearts and imagination of the British people. His final victory – after a long series of naval victories – at Trafalgar in 1805 when he decisively defeated French naval power but at the price of his own life had every element of drama inherent in the event. Several lives of Nelson had appeared after his death, but none had conveyed the quality of the hero's person or described in succinct form the great sea battles in which he had played decisive roles. Southey in the preface to his *Life* set forth his purpose and plan:

> Many lives of Nelson have been written. One is yet wanting, clear and concise enough to become a manual for the young sailor, which he may carry about with him, till he has treasured up the example in his memory and his heart. In attempting such a work, I shall write the eulogy of our great naval hero; for the best eulogy of Nelson is the faithful history of his actions; the best history, that which shall relate them most perspicuously.

Southey's biography was an expansion of a biographical essay which he had written for the *Quarterly Review* for the issue of February, 1810. This article was based upon James Stanier Clarke's and John McArthur's *Life*, a two-volume biography containing numerous documents and weighing twenty-one pounds. John Murray, the publisher of the *Quarterly*, was pleased with the article and recognized not only Southey's gift for biography but also the timeliness of the subject and suggested that the article be expanded into a book. This commission was one of the happiest of such assignments Southey was to receive and is a tribute to the insight and encouragement that a publisher can give an author. Most of the materials Southey needed were in Clarke and McArthur, but he also used to advantage the account of Dr William Beatty, the surgeon who attended Nelson at Trafalgar. Other works that he used were a biography by James Harrison, written under the patronage of Lady Hamilton, and travel books by William Coxe, Sir John Carr, and A. A. Feldborg for information about the scenes of some of the naval actions.

Southey was ideally suited for writing the biography. His clear and lucid style had by 1813 been perfected by a long apprenticeship for the reviews, and Murray's commission restricted Southey's tendency to digress so that he could not indulge his wish to explore interesting byways. He was furthermore a genuine and sincere admirer of Nelson so that he could narrate Nelson's career with generous enthusiasm. The fact that his brother Tom had been a lieutenant in the navy and had been present in many important naval battles had long given Southey a special interest and partiality for the navy. Then, too, his deep conviction that Napoleon and France must be defeated at all costs made him look upon Nelson as a national hero and even as a latter-day St George.

Southey's *Life of Nelson* contains approximately one hundred thousand words and is divided into nine chapters. The facts of Nelson's life are arranged chronologically with an emphasis upon his public career. Southey was unacquainted with any of the principals so that he relied upon published sources. The materials in Clarke and McArthur were abundant, and his task was that of the professional writer who must select the significant and narrate his story in a style that would be intelligible to the layman. Southey had a great advantage with his subject since the public was well aware of the great series of Nelson's victories: Cape St Vincent in 1797; the Egyptian victory at Aboukir Bay in 1798; Copenhagen in 1801; and last and greatest of all, the final victory off Cape Trafalgar in 1805. It was this side of Nelson's life and of the remarkable man who had made such victories possible that the public wished to read. Of Nelson's personal life Southey said no more than was necessary. Nelson's attachment to Lady Hamilton was public knowledge, as was his separation from his wife. Southey did not approve of this aspect of Nelson's life and said as little as possible about it. He also expressed disapproval of Nelson's share in the execution of Prince Caraccioli at Naples. These were blots upon the character of an otherwise noble man, and Southey had no wish to dwell upon them nor to explore the psychological reasons. Nelson's wholehearted devotion to duty, his patriotism, and his striving for glory in the best and most honorable sense of the word more than balanced any defects in his personal life.

The *Nelson* does not lend itself to quotation. The work needs to be read as a piece and then the special quality of Nelson's magnetic charm comes through to the reader. The detailed descriptions of the battles convey to the reader the sensation that he is really there and a consciousness of the presence of Nelson in all that happens. Southey may not always be the master of every nautical term or understand the finer points of naval tactics and strategy, but he is able to describe the naval engagement with the proper blend of excitement and apprehension for the average reader who is likewise ignorant of military tactics and strategy.

The reasons for the success and the continued popularity of the book are many and obvious. Southey's sympathy and admiration for Nelson were clearly apparent, and perhaps without realizing the fact, his own life had certain parallels with Nelson's. Both Southey and Nelson believed in and practiced devotion to duty, both shared a Francophobia and a firm conviction that Napoleon and France must be defeated if Britain were to survive. And even as Nelson wished for military glory, so did Southey strive for a literary fame and glory. There was, of course, much more on Nelson's side that had appealed to the public. His spectacular victories were the type of public display which everyone could understand and applaud, and with every victory Nelson came to embody his country. There was in him – as for no other man of the age – and in his career, an epic quality: he was the national hero who in the final scene loses his own life in the great national victory at Trafalgar in a triumph of good over evil. This quality comes through in Southey's biography. The hour had called for a hero and one had appeared. The nineteenth-century cult of the hero and Carlyle's *Heroes and Hero-Worship* were yet to come, but Southey in *The Life of Nelson* had already provided the public with a biography of one.

The Life of Wesley

Southey's *Life of Wesley*, generally considered as second to his *Life of Nelson*, is not only a life of Welsey but also a history of the rise of Methodism. Wesley was one of the influential men of the eighteenth century and as remarkable for the quality of his character as for the great movement which he inspired and led. Southey follows Wesley from his early days, his life at Oxford, his sojourn in the United States, his visit to the Moravians in Germany, and the various struggles with his early followers. Southey was able to use Wesley's journal and often lets Wesley tell his story in his own words. Unfortunately, Southey wrote not only a biography, but incorporated into the work a history of the entire movement. He was not, however, a theologian and not professionally equipped to discuss metaphysical and theological points, nor quite able to understand the complex religious personality of Wesley. A great deal of the spirit of the Methodists and of Wesley was alien to Southey's religious temperament. But whatever the faults of the biography it did the memory of Wesley a great service. Clearly written and well organized, the book was based upon wide reading and research and was infinitely superior to any biography of Wesley that had yet appeared. It was a tribute to one of the great men of the eighteenth century, and it made the reading public, apart from the Methodists, aware of Wesley's great qualities.

The Life of Wesley has had many admirers, but none more eloquent than S. T. Coleridge, who spoke of it as 'the book more often in my hands than any other in my ragged book-regiment. . . . How many and many an hour of self-oblivion do I owe to this Life of Wesley.' The marginalia in Coleridge's copy of his *Wesley* were incorporated in the third edition of the work (1846) and are also found in FitzGerald's edition (1925). Others too have praised the work. Edward Dowden spoke of a 'lucidity and a perfect exposition such as we rarely find outside a French memoir.'

A few sentences from Southey's last paragraph will give something of the style and flavor of the biography as well as giving his attitude towards Wesley and the Methodists. Southey speaks of him as:

> a man of great views, great energy, and great virtues. That he awakened a zealous spirit, not only in his own community, but in a Church which needed something to quicken it, is acknowledged by the members of that Church itself; that he encouraged enthusiasm and extravagance, lent a ready ear to false and impossible relations, and spread superstition as well as piety, would hardly be denied by the candid and judicious among his own people. In its immediate effects, the powerful principle of religion which he and his preachers diffused, has reclaimed many from a course of sin, has supported many in poverty, sickness, and affliction, and has imparted to many a triumphant joy in death.

Finally, Southey looked forward to the time when the Methodists would return to the Church:

> The obstacles to this are surely not insuperable, perhaps not so difficult as they may appear. And were this effected, John Wesley would then be ranked, not only among the most remarkable and influential men of his age, but among the great benefactors of his country and his kind.

Biography and Edition of William Cowper

In the autumn of 1833 the publishing firm of Baldwin and Cradock approached Southey with the request that he undertake an edition of the works of William Cowper for the sum of one thousand guineas. During the next two years Southey assiduously collected materials from every source open to him and succeeded in gaining access to many unpublished letters and manuscripts. The first volume of the fifteen-volume edition appeared in 1836 and the final volume in 1837. Of most interest is the life of Cowper in the first three volumes, a very full and detailed account of the author's life, friends, and works. Southey's method of arrangement is chronological, and he interrupts his own narrative with excerpts from Cowper's correspondence and from his poetry to illustrate biographical points. Southey had always been an admirer of Cowper's poetry and had sympathized with the difficulties of the poet's life. His own distrust of the Calvinistic evangelicalism of Cowper's friend, the Reverend John Newton, gave him ample opportunity to explore the unfortunate and distressing effects which this form of Christianity had upon one of Cowper's temperament. Cowper's ultimate madness of which Southey was forced to write came at a most unfortunate time for him, for it was during the composition of this work upon Cowper that Mrs Southey was suffering from a hopeless and incurable mental illness. 'When I undertook the task of writing Cowper's life I little apprehended that it would be my lot to have a case of madness under my own constant observation' (*New Letters*, vol. 2, p. 426).

In the course of writing Cowper's life Southey gives a full account of the literary scene in London and of Cowper's associates during his early years: Bonnell Thornton, George Colman, Robert Lloyd, Charles Churchill. In some ways the most interesting chapter of Southey's biography of Cowper is the twelfth chapter (in volume 2) entitled 'Sketch of the Progress of English Poetry from Chaucer to Cowper.' An unfinished project of Southey had been a history of English literature or a continuation of Warton's history, and this chapter provides a glimpse of what that work might have been. For Southey the four great names in English poetry are Chaucer, Spenser, Shakespeare, and Milton. Much of his chapter is devoted to a discussion of versification, of the importance of Surrey, of the attempt to introduce classical metres into English poetry, and of the dissimilarities between poetry written in English and in Spanish or Italian. His view, however, of the century before Cowper and of himself is most interesting, for here he finds little to praise. The Restoration which had brought about a corruption of manners found this corruption reflected in its literature.

Inflated tragedies, comedies so grossly indecent that, if it were
possible for them now to be brought upon the stage, they
would be driven off with hootings of execration, lewd tales in
verse, songs, epigrams, and satires, in which ribaldry or
malignity served for condiment; occasional verses, the best of
which deserved to be remembered no longer than while the
occasion which called them forth was recent; – for such poetry,
fit and large audience might be found, but for any thing better,
the public, or as it was then called, the Town, had neither
inclination nor capacity. The age from Dryden to Pope is the
worst age of English poetry (vol. 2, p. 138).

When he comes to a discussion of Pope, Southey can only quote
Bishop Hurd's comment that 'Pope had shut the door against poetry,'
and could add that 'if Pope shut the door, Cowper opened it' (vol.
2, p. 142). Nor was Pope's influence beneficial for poetry. 'That
school has produced versifiers in abundance, but no poet' (vol. 2,
p. 143).

Blank verse he considered as 'perfectly in accord with the genius of
our language' and the use at the Restoration of rhymed forms adapted
from the French was but another bit of evidence of the degenerated
taste introduced at that time. Dryden did not aim at a high mark, but
excelled as no other poet before or since in satire and the didactic, but
despite his excellences, 'there was nothing for the imagination, nothing
for the feelings' (vol. 2, p. 139). Pope's influence on subsequent poets
was mischievous, but this mischief was effected by his translation of
Homer – 'no other work in the language so greatly vitiated the diction
of English poetry.'

This edition still stands as an important work for the study of Cowper
since his complete works have not been subsequently edited in a single
publication. The first three volumes contain the life of Cowper, the
fourth through seventh his correspondence, volumes eight through
ten his poems, and the eleventh through fourteenth his translation of
Homer, and the fifteenth includes additional letters and seven prose
essays. Southey planned two additional volumes of Cowperiana
devoted to the literary history of Cowper's family and friends, but
these were not published because of the bankruptcy of the publishers,
Baldwin and Cradock. Southey's fifteen-volume edition of Cowper
was reprinted in eight volumes in the Bohn Library in 1853–5.

Southey in his life of Cowper was writing a biography and not literary criticism, but it was necessary to make statements concerning Cowper's poems. Southey does much in describing the circumstances of the composition of these poems and quotes appropriate passages from Cowper's letters by way of illustration, but he does not make sharp critical observations on the poems and never gives the reader any close critical analysis of particular passages in the poems. A few of his remarks upon *The Task* will show the nature of his commentary.

> The Task was at once descriptive, moral, and satirical. The descriptive parts every where bore evidence of a thoughtful mind and a gentle spirit, as well as of an observant eye; and the moral sentiment which pervaded them, gave a charm in which descriptive poetry is often found wanting. . . . He was in a happier state of mind, and in more cheerful circumstances when he began the Task: it was therefore less acrimonious. Its satire is altogether free from personality; it is the satire not of a sour and discontented spirit, but of a benevolent though melancholy mind; and the melancholy was not of a kind to affect artificial gloom and midnight musings, but rather to seek and find relief in sunshine, in the beauties of nature, in books and leisure, in solitary or social walks, and in the comforts of a quiet fire-side (vol. 2, pp. 183-4).

Southey approved of the presence of the poet in the poem; he would not have appreciated the critical point of view that a poem should be read apart from any consideration of the author. In reading *The Task* 'the reader feels that the poet is continually present; he becomes intimately acquainted with him, and this it is which gives to this delightful poem its unity and its peculiar charm' (vol. 2, p. 185).

Short Biographies

Although Southey's book-length biographies are well known, he also wrote a series of short biographies for the *Quarterly* based upon a new biography or a recently edited journal or memoir. His *Life of Nelson* grew out of such a biographical article, but there are several other such brief biographies in the *Quarterly*: William Huntington S. S. (Sinner Saved), an entertaining account of a fanatical preacher (1821); a sketch of the Duke of Marlborough (1820), a glorification of the Duke as a model patriot and statesman; John Evelyn (1818), the model of an English gentleman. Among others in the *Quarterly* were sketches of Cromwell (1821), the Chevalier Bayard (1825), John Oberlin (1831), Admiral Howe (1838), and Thomas Telford (1838). The best of these small-scale biographies may well be that of the Chevalier Bayard, whose memoir the twenty-three-year-old Sara Coleridge had just translated. Here Southey was able to indulge his love of chivalry and the Middle Ages in depicting the exemplary life of the famous *Chevalier sans peur et sans reproche*. A quick glance at the essays shows Southey's method. He first identifies Bayard and then commends the translator for good work in making this memoir available for the first time: *The Right Joyous and Pleasant History of the Feats, Gests and Prowesses of the Chevalier Bayard By the Loyal Servant* (London, 1825). Southey next gives a chronological account of the life of Pierre du Terrail (the Chevalier's name), born in 1476 of a good family in Dauphiny and renowned for brave, military feats. Southey's narrative selects a series of anecdotes designed to show Bayard's independence, bravery, honor, and generosity. Bayard lived during the last days of chivalry when it was still possible for a knight to distinguish himself by his personal valor, but gunpowder – as the Chevalier recognized – was soon to change the old ways. Bayard's campaigns in Italy showed him to be not only skilful in direct combat and in the conduct of sieges, but generous to his adversaries, to his captives, and liberal with the ransoms he received, rewarding his associates to such an extent that often nothing remained for himself. The concluding paragraph clearly states the lesson of Bayard's life:

> If he had merely won victories for France greater than those of Turenne or Villars, he would have conferred less honour upon his country, and rendered less service to it, than he has done by the example of his personal character. . . . We are glad therefore that English readers may now become as familiar with the history of the Chevalier Bayard as they were with his name; and a wish may be expressed that the French in return would make themselves acquainted with the English knight, *sans peur et sans reproche*, Sir Philip Sidney (vol. 32, p. 397).

Southey's biographical essay upon John Evelyn, the seventeenth-century diarist whose diary was first published in 1818, can also be read with pleasure. Evelyn's career as scholar and country gentleman was congenial to Southey's own temperament, and he could describe Evelyn's life with total sympathy. This is Southey's conclusion:

All persons, indeed, may find in his character something for imitation; but for an English gentleman he is the perfect model. Neither to solicit public offices, nor to shun them, but when they are conferred to execute their duties diligently, conscientiously and fearlessly; to have no amusements but such as being laudable as well as innocent, are healthful alike for the mind and for the body, and in which, while the passing hour is beguiled, a store of delightful recollection is laid up; to be the liberal encourager of literature and the arts; to seek for true and permanent enjoyment by the practice of the household virtues – the only course by which it can be found; to enlarge the sphere of existence backward by means of learning through all time, and forward by means of faith through all eternity, – behold the fair ideal of human happiness (vol. 19, p. 54).

Southey's article on Cromwell shows his ability to appreciate that leader's dynamic qualities even though he had to censure his actions. Cromwell was for Southey a military despot who had brought suffering and anarchy to the three kingdoms, but who was in many ways a credible and admirable individual. Like Macbeth, to whom Southey compares him, he discovered his mistakes after his success. Cromwell, always in fear of his life, 'would have governed constitutionally, mildly, mercifully, liberally, if he could have followed the impulses of his own heart, and the wishes of his better mind!' (vol. 25, pp. 345–46). Southey finally calls him this 'least flagitious of usurpers.' Southey usually is at his best when he can fully sympathize with the subject about whom he is writing, but the Cromwell essay reveals him as capable of writing with a professional detachment that he had learned in the hard school of reviewing.

Southey also wrote other short biographies as introductions to editions of works that he edited or sponsored. These are the lives of Henry Kirke White (1808), John Bunyan (1830), the lives of the uneducated poets as the preface to John Jones's *Attempts in Verse* (1831), and Isaac Watts (1834). An interesting volume could be made by collecting several of these biographies since most of them are available only in the form in which they originally appeared.

5

Autobiography

Letters

Portions of autobiography can be found in almost everything that Southey wrote in that his attitudes, interests, beliefs, and prejudices are always present. But his correspondence, his travel journals, his *Common-Place Book*, and the greater part of *The Doctor*, that mixture of fiction and autobiography, clearly belong to the autobiographical category. Much of the *Letters from England* is directly from Southey's own experience, and he often forgets that the book is supposedly from the pen of a young Spaniard and writes in his own person. Similarly, his *Colloquies* in their descriptions of his pastimes, of the setting of his home, Greta Hall, and of the routine of his days given to study and writing in his library contain much autobiography. It has seemed best, however, to discuss these last two works under the heading of social and political criticism. But the reader of Southey should be prepared to find autobiography everywhere in his writing.

Southey's letters provide the best picture of Southey as a person, for it is in his letters that he is most completely himself. The materials are voluminous, and the problem in a discussion of the letters is one of limitation and classification. Southey enjoyed writing letters, and he seems to have answered most of his letters promptly. His most extensive correspondence was between his two oldest friends, Grosvenor Bedford and Charles Wynn, with whom he maintained a life-long exchange of letters. John Rickman was another correspondent with whom he maintained a life-long exchange, as was William Taylor of Norwich, John May, Charles Danvers, and his brother Tom. With his literary friends, however, the exchange of correspondence was subject to more interruptions and a longer interval between letters. His correspondence with Coleridge was lively enough for several years during the first part of his life, but lagged; Wordsworth did not care for epistolizing, and the nearness of their residences made the personal exchange of visits and information a substitute for letters. Landor and Scott were valued correspondents upon literary matters. Letters of business were numerous, but Southey's letters to John Murray, unlike Byron's, were confined to business and not personal anecdote. Southey's family received many letters from him, especially his two brothers Henry Herbert and Tom, and some of his fullest letters describing his travels and social activities when away from home were addressed to his wife. His letters, although few in number, to his children and his nephew Hartley Coleridge are delightful. The letters to his women correspondents reveal another side of his personality. Those to Mary Barker are lively and humorous in tone reflecting her own lively and humorous traits, those to Caroline Bowles are kind and encouraging, and those in later years to Mrs Septimus Hodson and Mrs Thomas Hughes respond to the kindly and intelligent interest these ladies took in his personal and literary projects. A reading of a few representative letters is the best way to savor and estimate Southey as letter writer.

Southey was as fluent in letter writing as in other areas of composition. His first letters were long verse epistles to his schoolboy friends, but these need not detain us. His first letters of interest are those which he wrote from Oxford in 1793-4. These give a full picture of the life of a serious young man, apprehensive over his future situation in life, unable to accept the idea of taking holy orders, critical of his elders, especially as represented by the fellows and be-wigged masters of the colleges, absorbed in writing his first long poem *Joan of Arc*, but still finding plenty of time for social gatherings in the rooms of his friends and for walking trips and outings during the good weather. He says very little about collegiate studies, but a great deal about his own reading, and speculates about what he might do in place of entering the Church: first, he thought of medicine, then of a place in a public office, next of emigration to America, and with the advent of the visiting Coleridge from Cambridge of pantisocracy with its vision of an ideal community in Pennsylvania on the banks of the Susquehannah.

Years later Southey's position as an established author resulted in the receipt of letters from would-be authors, to whom he responded courteously but discouragingly. Henry Kirke White, a young poet whom Southey had reviewed and advised, died at an early age and Southey edited a selection of White's poetry, earning for himself and for White a considerable measure of fame because the volume attracted

attention from the evangelical reading public. Caroline Bowles wrote
him in 1818 about the publication of a poem and received a polite
letter with suggestions for its improvement. From this letter a friendship developed that ended twenty years later in their marriage.
Charlotte Brontë is the most famous of these aspiring authors who
wrote Southey for advice. Her unusual name made him suspect that it
might be a pseudonym. He commended her on the quality of her
verses but warned her of the disappointments awaiting all who undertake a literary life and urged her not to neglect her proper duties in
life:

> But do not suppose that I disparage the gift which you possess;
> nor that I would discourage you from exercising it. I only exhort
> you so to think of it, and so to use it, as to render it conducive
> to your own permanent good. Write poetry for its own sake;
> not in a spirit of emulation, and with a view to celebrity: the
> less you aim at that, the more likely you will be to deserve, and
> finally to obtain it (*Letters of Robert Southey: A Selection*, ed.
> M. H. FitzGerald, Oxford, 1912, p. 510, from Mrs Gaskell's
> *Life of Charlotte Brontë*).

Southey concluded his letter by signing himself as 'Your true friend'
even though she might think him 'an ungracious adviser.' Charlotte
Brontë was deeply touched with this letter and replied with every
expression of thankfulness giving him an account of her life and of
her family and assuring him that Charlotte Brontë was her real name.

Southey often gave bits of advice to his younger correspondents on
matters of style and the collection of materials. On the subject of style
his counsel can be summed up in the phrase 'Don't worry.'

> My advice to a young writer is, that he should weigh well what
> he says, and not be anxious concerning *how* he says it: that his
> first object should be to express his meaning as perspicuously, his
> second as briefly as he can, and in this everything is included
> (To Henry Taylor, December 31, 1825, *Life*, vol. 5, pp. 240–1).

He once wrote his brother Henry Herbert a long letter on the subject
of record-keeping or note-taking when his brother was contemplating
the writing of a history of the crusades. The letter, too long for quotation, may be summarized. Southey recommended a notebook in
which the best original author is used as the basis for the account. The
opposite page should be left blank for adding to the basic account and

with further provision for adding to the additions. Miscellaneous notes were to be kept on separate pieces of paper, numbered, and indexed. Southey then listed several useful titles and recommended reading every traveler who had written upon Syria, Egypt, or Palestine. He warned his brother not to be dismayed by the sight of a large quarto but to 'read on manfully.' As for style he repeated the advice he always gave. 'A Welsh triad might comprehend all the rules for style. Say what you have to say as *perspicuously* as possible, as *briefly* as possible, and as *rememberably* as possible, and take no other thought about it' (August 17, 1809, *Letters*, vol. 2, pp. 156–8).

Unless Southey is writing upon matters of business or expressing his concern over political and national affairs, his letters usually have a genial and even humorous undertone. A few are written in a playful spirit and are filled with jokes and nonsense. How well such letters, after so many years, come through is hard to say. The private joke between friends does not always travel well. Grosvenor Bedford received most of them since Southey wrote to him often as a relief from the serious business of the day. On occasion he even wrote Bedford in Latin – a very bad Latin, it is true, with many English words disguised by Latin endings: 'Ubi Diabolus es tu Bedford? Ubi est nova domus Brixtoniensis? ubi diabolus est mea pensio?' And the letter concluded with a Latin pun on Grosvenor's name: 'Ego sum somnus-y, quia est post decem horologium. Bona nox mi Nemus-nec'* (*New Letters*, vol. 1, pp. 453–4). He also wrote humorous letters in French to John King, a physician of Swiss origin, living in Bristol (*Letters*, vol. 1, pp. 186–9). Miss Mary Barker was also a recipient of a few nonsensical letters from Southey. On August 5, 1804 he wrote a letter consisting mostly of questions:

> Why have you not set out for Keswick? Why have you not told us when you mean to set out? Do you mean to set out at all? Do you ever mean to come? Do you never mean to come? This is the last time of asking? Are you in Staffordshire? Is this letter directed right? Is it directed wrong? How ought it to be directed? How can I tell how to direct it? Do you like to be asked questions? Do you admire the catechistical form of epistolising? (*Letters*, vol. 1, p. 283).

* 'Where the devil are you, Bedford? Where is your new Brixton house? Where the devil is my pension?' . . . 'I am sleepy, because it is after ten o'clock. Good night my Grove-nor.'

After more questioning the letter concludes with a series of invitations based upon the word 'Come' printed in a variety of sizes and with appropriate exclamation points. Miss Barker, a friend from Portuguese days, later resided in Keswick.

Southey is at his best when in the course of a letter he describes a small group, sketching in lightly the scene and characters, and reveals the tension just beneath the polite veneer of good social manners. Jack Simmons in his *Southey* (p. 117) chose for analysis Southey's description of the evening he spent with his uncle Thomas Southey as a vivid example of this power. Another equally good is his account of Colonel Peachey's dinner when Southey met for the first and only time Lord Somerville, a distant cousin, who had inherited estates that Southey had supposed were entailed on him should Lord Somerville die without heirs. No notice was taken at the dinner of the connection between the two although both were well aware of it.

Our neighbour Colonel Peachy invited us lately to meet Lord Somerville at dinner. Both Harry and I and Danvers, who was of the party, conceived a strong dislike to him. He was very amusing and certainly does not want talents, but his mind and his manners are coarse and vulgar; he is a nondescript mulish compound of butcher and courtier, both bad breeds, and the mixture worse than either. I liked him so little as to be glad that he offered no kind of civility on taking leave, which might have made it necessary for me to call at his London door. From hence he went into Scotland, and there saw his neighbour Walter Scott, the poet of the Border, who was on the point of coming here to visit Wordsworth and me. To Scott he spoke of the relationship with us. He said of me and Wordsworth that however we might have got into good company he might depend upon it we were still Jacobines at heart, and that he believed he had been instrumental in having us looked after in Somersetshire. This refers to a spy who was sent down to Stowey to look after Coleridge and Wordsworth: the fellow after trying to tempt the country people to tell lies, could collect nothing more than that the gentlemen used to walk a good deal upon the coast, and that they were what they called poets. He got drunk at the inn, and told his whole errand and history, but we did not till now know who was the main mover. If you recollect how well this dirty poaching for perjury assorts with his views upon

John Southey's money, you will be able to form a good estimate of his Lordships honourable morality (*New Letters*, vol. 1, p. 392, corrected from the misleading and garbled version in *Life*, vol. 2, p. 343).

Lord Somerville is the subject of a complimentary sketch by Scott, who admired him for his interest in improving the breeding of sheep. In 1802 Lord Somerville, who had been on good terms with Southey's wealthy uncle, John Southey, quarrelled with him and thus lost the prospect of inheriting that property, no part of which ever came to Southey. What share Lord Somerville had in having the Home Office send down a spy will probably never be known, but his own admission suggests that personal malice against Southey and his friends was present. It is not often that anyone has the opportunity which Southey had of meeting for the one and only time an individual whom he has suspected of being his enemy and of finding his worst fears confirmed. Southey, it may be noted here, discovered after Lord Somerville's death in 1819 that the claim to the entailed estates was so tenuous as not to be worth litigation.

Southey's descriptions of most persons whom he met are good humored, and he was usually amused by what he saw and heard. His description of Amelia Opie, a very minor author and a Quaker, in a letter of October 15, 1826, is such an example, as she stopped at Keswick on her way to Lowther Castle:

> in stiffer garb and more primitive bonnet than when I saw her at Norwich, and corrupting the King's English with more malice prepense. She went from hence to Lowther; but though she *thou'd* and *thee'd* them with great intrepidity, I am told that the sinful word Lady slipped not unfrequently from her lips; and that when Rogers, as if to put her young virtue to the proof, said things and told stories at which she ought not to have laughed, the temptation was sometimes so strong that she was obliged to stuff her handkerchief into her mouth, and still the struggling titter came forth, the old Eve prevailing in the contest. I like her in spite of her Quakerism, nay, perhaps the better for it (*Letters*, vol. 4, p. 36).

Southey has left no specific description of Wordsworth, but he has recorded in many places his high estimate of Wordsworth's character and genius. In 1814 he recognized the power of the *Excursion* and set down what was to be his final judgment of Wordsworth:

I have known him nearly twenty years, and, for about half that time, intimately. The strength and the character of his mind you see in the *Excursion*, and his life does not belie his writings, for, in every relation of life, and every point of view, he is a truly exemplary and admirable man. In conversation he is powerful beyond any of his contemporaries; and, as a poet, – I speak not from the partiality of friendship, nor because we have been so absurdly held up as both writing upon one concerted system of poetry, but with the most deliberate exercise of impartial judgement whereof I am capable, when I declare my full conviction that posterity will rank him with Milton (To Bernard Barton, December 19, 1814, *Life*, vol. 4, p. 91).

The death of Miss Sara Hutchinson, Mrs Wordsworth's sister, brought forth a tribute that indicated the thirty-year intimacy between the two families. In Southey's words, she had for over thirty years:

partaken of all the joys and sorrows of this family, and whose loss is, to my poor daughters, the severest that could have befallen them out of their own nearest and dearest kin. She had lived a life of single blessedness, living about with her friends and relations, each wishing to keep her longer, for she was a comfort and a blessing to them all. . . . She loved us dearly, – no one indeed could love us better, and very few indeed knew us so well (To Mrs Hughes, July 1, 1835, *Letters*, vol. 4, pp. 408–9).

In his letters to his oldest friends Southey was not diffident about expressing to them the value he placed upon their friendship and for their good offices to him. The best of these is his letter to Wynn of January 27, 1828 on the fortieth anniversary of their meeting at Westminster School:

It is now forty years since you and I first met in Dean's Yard! To me it proved the most beneficial meeting which ever befell me; and had I followed any of the ordinary walks of life, it would doubtless have been the means of advancing me in any profession to the heights of professional ambition. Perhaps, of the whole three hundred who then composed the eternal body puerile of Westminster, there were no two whose future course and condition in society might have been more truly predicted from their dispositions, inclinations, and the circumstances in which they were placed. But had it not been for your aid I should have been irretrievably wrecked when I ran upon the shoals, with all sail set, in the very outset of my voyage. You have been the means of putting many in the way of fortune; but you never can have rendered to any one a more essential benefit, nor one that has been more deeply and thankfully felt. I have, I trust, enough of the spirit of independence, but I have none of its pride. Men are as much the better for the good offices which they receive as for those which they bestow (*Letters*, vol. 4, pp. 87–8).

The reference here is, of course, to the annual pension of £160 which Wynn granted Southey when he became of age.

To Joseph Cottle, the publisher of his first books, he expressed his appreciation on several occasions. On April 20, 1808 he wrote:

Do you suppose, Cottle, that I have forgotten those true and most essential acts of friendship which you showed me when I stood most in need of them? Your house was my house when I had no other. The very money with which I bought my wedding-ring and paid my marriage fees, was supplied by you. It was with your sisters I left Edith during my six months' absence, and for the six months' after my return it was from you that I received, week by week, the little on which we lived, till I was enabled to live by other means. . . . Sure I am, there never was a more generous or a kinder heart than yours; and you will believe me when I add, that there does not live that man upon earth whom I remember with more gratitude and more affection. My head throbs and my eyes burn with these recollections (*Life*, vol. 3, pp. 136–7).

Such a tribute did not mean that Southey was blind to Cottle's very real and very apparent shortcomings. Thus he wrote Caroline Bowles in 1837 on the publication of Cottle's recollections of Coleridge and Southey, as unreliable and as inaccurate a book as was ever published:

That you should like Cottle's book, dear Caroline, is as impossible as it would be for you to dislike Cottle himself, if you knew him as I know him; but unless you knew him thus thoroughly, you could not believe that such simple-heartedness and such inordinate vanity were to be found in the same person (Bowles, p. 351).

This brief sketch of Southey's letters may well conclude with a description of one of the most charming groups of letters: those to children. When Southey's nephew, Hartley Coleridge, known also by his nickname of Job, was eleven, he and his mother made a long trip to London and the west of England, and Southey wrote him a long eight-paragraph letter telling him of the news at Greta Hall. The letter is perfectly adapted to the interests and understanding of a child and has just the right blend of humor and seriousness that would appeal to Hartley. After explaining his delay in writing Southey devotes a paragraph to one of the cats:

> Bona Marietta hath had kittens; they were remarkably ugly, all taking after their father Thomas, who there is reason to believe was either uncle or grandsire to Bona herself, the prohibited degrees of consanguinity which you will find at the end of the Bible not being regarded by cats. As I have never been able to persuade this family that catlings, fed for the purpose and smothered with onions, would be rabbits to all eatable purposes, Bona Marietta's ugly progeny no sooner came into the world than they were sent out of it; the river nymph Greta conveyed them to the river god Derwent, and if neither the eels nor the ladies of the lake have taken a fancy to them on their way, Derwent hath consigned them to the Nereids. You may imagine them converted into sea-cats by favour of Neptune, and write an episode to be inserted in Ovid's Metamorphoses. Bona bore the loss patiently, and is in good health and spirits. I fear that if you meet with any of the race of Mrs Rowe's cat at Ottery, you will forget poor Marietta. Don't bite your arm, Job.

The letter then gives news of an outing, a new boat, plantings of trees in the garden, of the loss of four chickens to a kite, mentions Edith May and Herbert Southey, the weather, and the dog Dapper. 'Your friend Dapper, who is, I believe, your god-dog, is in good health, though he grows every summer graver than the last.' The letter concludes with remembrances to Mr Thomas Poole, a message to his father about some books, and a long conclusion enclosing messages of love from every one in the household (June 13, 1807, *Life*, vol. 3, pp. 100–3).

In 1820 Southey received the honorary degree of LL.D. from Oxford University. To his three youngest daughters, Bertha, Kate, and Isabel, then between eight and eleven, he related the event in a mixture of quite serious – and also very careful – description of the event with teasing banter at the conclusion. The scene in the theater and the assembly and the process of LL.D.-ing were given in detail:

> Oh Bertha, Kate, and Isabel, if you had seen me that day! I
>   was like other *issimis*, dressed in a great robe of the finest
>   scarlet cloth, with sleeves of rose-coloured silk, and I had in
>   my hand a black velvet cap like a beef-eater, for the use of which
>   dress I paid one guinea for the day. Dr Phillimore, who was an
>   old school-fellow of mine, and a very good man, took me by the
>   hand in my turn, and presented me; upon which there was a
>   great clapping of hands and huzzaing at my name.

And in the concluding paragraph Southey told them:

> Little girls, you know it might be proper for me, now, to wear
> a large wig, and to be called Doctor Southey, and to become
> very severe, and leave off being a comical papa.

But then he added that:

> I shall not come down in a wig, neither shall I wear my robes at
> home (*Life*, vol. 5, pp. 38–41).

Not all Southey's letters to children were light in tone. In 1826 Isabel Southey, a girl of fourteen, died suddenly, and Southey's letter (July 19, 1826) to his three surviving daughters, Edith May, Bertha, and Katharine, is a moving and eloquent document. The letter is too long for quotation, but Southey reminded them:

> This is but the first trial of many such which are in store for
> you. Who may be summoned next is known only to the All-wise
> Disposer of all things. Some of you must have to mourn for
> others; some one for all the rest. It may be the will of God
> that I should follow more of my children to the grave; or in the
> ordinary course of nature and happiest issue, they may see their
> parents depart. . . . We must all depart when our time comes, –
> all to be re-united in a better state of existence, where we shall
> part no more.

Southey then reminded them that our task is to prepare ourselves for that state, not by renouncing innocent pleasures, but by correcting faults and improving dispositions:

I can truly say that my desire has ever been to make your childhood happy, as I would fain make your youth, and pray that God would make the remainder of your days. And for the dear child who is departed, God knows that I never heard her name mentioned, nor spoke, nor thought of her, without affection and delight.

Southey made a copy of this letter in his own hand for each of the daughters so that, although they will read the letter now with grief, they will later 'feel grateful for this proof of love' (*Life*, vol. 5, pp. 255–9).

If there be an anthologist of letters addressed to children, he should certainly include a few of those written by Southey.

Journals

Although Southey's life was largely spent at the writing desk, he enjoyed traveling, and made many tours, both long and short. As a young man he made walking trips from Bristol, Oxford, and London. In 1795 and again in 1800 he traveled and resided in Portugal and Spain, for six months on his first visit, and for a year and a half on the second. The Napoleonic wars had effectively closed most of Europe to British travelers, but in 1815 Southey visited Belgium and the field of Waterloo, kept a journal, and wrote *The Poet's Pilgrimage to Waterloo*. In 1817 he again visited the Continent, making a long circuit through Paris, where he called upon Wordsworth's daughter Caroline, and reached Switzerland and northern Italy. During the summers of 1825 and 1826 he visited the Low Countries, where he made the friendship of the Dutch poet, Willem Bilderdijk, and his wife, the translator of *Roderick*. His last trip to France occurred in the summer of 1838 in the company of H. C. Robinson and other friends. There were also trips within Britain – other than the long circuits he often took between Keswick and London – notably his visit in 1819 to the Highlands of Scotland and the Caledonian Canal in the company of John Rickman and Thomas Telford, the designer of the Canal, and during the winter of 1836-37 his long circuit with his son Cuthbert to Bristol and the West of England, where he visited for the last time the haunts of his boyhood and young manhood. Southey recorded these trips in varying detail in the letters which he wrote to family and friends, but during several of these trips he kept, in addition, careful journals.

Several of these have been posthumously published: *Journal of a Residence in Portugal 1800–1801 and a Visit to France 1838* (1960); *Journal of a Tour in the Netherlands in the Autumn of 1815* (1902); *Journal of a Tour in Scotland in 1819* (1929); short journals of trips in England during 1799, 1800, and 1805 are in his *Common-Place Book* (fourth volume).

Of these journals the most consistently interesting and readable is that of the tour in Scotland. Written when Southey was at the height of his powers as a writer and in the full vigor of his health, the journal shows a continual delight and interest in everything seen and every person met. The tour – from August 17 to October 1 – was in the company of his old friend John Rickman and his family and the engineer Thomas Telford, who had designed many roads, bridges, and the famous Caledonian Canal. The tour for Telford and Rickman was an official trip of inspection, and as a consequence the party received many courtesies from local officials and lairds. Although Southey and Telford had never met before, they were immediately upon friendly terms. 'There is so much intelligence in his countenance, so much frankness, kindness and hilarity about him, flowing from the never-failing wellspring of a happy nature, that I was upon cordial terms with him in five minutes' (*Journal of a Tour in Scotland*, ed. C. H. Herford, London, 1929, p. 7). Southey's usual interests were not problems of engineering, but he eagerly picked up all that Telford told him, and the journal contains explicit accounts of the way in which roads were built, the problems encountered in erecting bridges, and the economic advantages that followed as a consequence of these improvements (pp. 54, 97, 116). Rickman – 'the strongest-headed and most sagacious man whom I have ever known' (p. 213) – understood the economic and statistical implications of what he saw, and it is evident how often his point of view is expressed in the journal entries. Southey infers the prosperity of a town by noting the quality of the roofs; the prosperity of the farming by the nature of the crops grown. It is better in Scotland to raise potatoes and vegetables than to try the difficult job of growing grain in order to have wheaten bread. The quality of this journal that places it above the level of the tourist interested only in the picturesque and the quaint detail is this awareness of the serious struggle for life in which the people were engaged. Because Southey was traveling in the company of knowledgeable and official persons this journal has a substance – and an importance for the general picture of Scottish life in 1819 – that it could not otherwise have had.

The journal, however, is not wanting in observations of a literary man. Southey is aware of the literary and historical associations of the places visited, is interested in the architecture of churches, ruined castles, and even stops to record inscriptions of monuments. He described the countryside through which they passed and seemed properly appreciative of what may be called 'romantic' scenery. His love of books is apparent by his regular visits to the bookshops, which he observed were more common in Scotland than in England, and made purchases which he noted. Even very small towns had one or more bookshops. He takes time to visit the tomb of Beattie, mentions Ossian, and is aware that Johnson and Boswell had preceded him in touring Scotland. Occasionally, he quotes Wordsworth. Southey willingly put up with the simple accommodation of the inns and objected only to filth and lack of cleanliness. His appetite throughout the tour was excellent, and he records with appreciation the fare, especially the breakfasts which often included salmon, finnan haddock, or herring. Whisky was regularly provided, on occasion even at breakfast.

Southey expressed his views on the changes taking place in Scotland in outspoken fashion. He much regretted the ruthless manner in which the Scottish landowners had expelled their tenants. The Marquess of Stafford's estates comprised two-fifths of the county of Sutherland and were being converted into large sheep-farms. His comment on the human consequences is:

> To transplant these people from their native mountain glens to the sea coast, and require them to become some cultivators, others fishermen, occupations to which they have never been accustomed – to expect a sudden and total change of habits in the existing generation, instead of gradually producing it in their children; to expel them by process of law from their black-houses, and if they demur in obeying the ejectment, to oust them by setting fire to these combustible tenements – this surely is as little defensible on the score of policy as of morals (p. 137).

His view of the landowners was by no means favorable because they abused their powers. It would have been far better to have kept the forfeited estates of the Highland chiefs in the hands of the Crown, leased them, or even sold them to strangers. Fifty large holders owned most of the Highlands and their 'object is to increase their revenue, and they care not by what means this is accomplished' (p. 209). One encouraging aspect of the Scottish scene is the large and benevolent presence of the government as it has built roads, bridges, canals, improved harbors and encouraged the development of fisheries and new forms of agriculture. These measures have immensely improved the lot of individuals and greatly increased the wealth of the country. Southey was a firm believer – unlike his critic Macaulay who opposed government 'interference' in economic matters – in the role of the government in taking steps to improve the quality of life for the people.

At the end of his trip Southey visited for a day Robert Owen's establishment at New Lanark, was hospitably received by Owen, and given a tour of the mill. It all reminded him of a convent in Portugal, or of a plantation in the West Indies, with the exception that the workers were free to leave. Although Southey admired and liked Owen personally, he thought there was a flaw in the arrangements because Owen viewed men as machines. 'I never regarded man as a machine; I never believed him to be merely a material being.' Owen, furthermore, 'keeps out of sight from others, and perhaps from himself, that his system, instead of aiming at perfect freedom, can only be kept in play by absolute power' (pp. 264–5).

This pleasant and most agreeable of journals ends happily with the return of the travellers to England, their farewells, and Southey's discovery on reaching Greta Hall that all was and had been well at home. To the connoisseur of the journal as a minor literary genre, to the lover of the Scottish scene, or to the student of Southey, the journal can be warmly recommended.

Common-Place Book

Southey's *Common-Place Book*, posthumously published (1849–51) and edited by J. W. Warter in four volumes, deserves a few words. This work surprisingly has had several reprintings both in England and in the United States. The collection of materials and the making of notes from his wide reading were favorite and habitual customs of Southey. In 1822 he described his method: 'Like those persons who frequent sales, and fill their houses with useless purchases, because they may want them some time or other; so am I ever making collections and storing up materials which may not come into use till the Greek Calends. And this I have been doing for five and twenty years!' (*Life*, vol. 5, p. 135). These materials were, of course, of practical use to him, and he drew upon them for his publications. Many entries can be traced to their resting places within his published works, but some were for works that were never to be published such as the history of the monastic orders and anecdotes for Espriella and *The Doctor* which were never used. The most interesting of the four series is the fourth one because here are found ideas for poems, personal notes and observations, and short journals of travels. The most notable journal is that of the trip with Coleridge during the summer of 1799 to the west of England, to Exeter, and to the ancestral seat of the Coleridges at Ottery St Mary.

A dilatory reader can leaf through the *Common-Place Book* and can never know what odd bit he may encounter. Seemingly no subject is untouched, but the literary, ecclesiastical, and historical predominate. A sample note on a Spanish poet will give a fair sample of Southey's manner in his notes:

> Gongora is the frog of the fable, his limbs are large, but it is a
> dropsy that has swollen them. You read him, and after you
> have unravelled the maze of his meaning, feel like one who has
> tired his jaws in cracking an empty nut (vol. 2, p. 209).

The Doctor

The Doctor, Southey's one attempt at fiction, had its beginning as early as 1805 when he suggested that Bedford write a book of nonsense and sent him a chapter for the proposed book. The first two volumes, however, did not appear until 1834. A third followed in 1835, a fourth in 1837, a fifth in 1838, and the two final volumes, edited by J. W. Warter, were published posthumously in 1847. Since Bedford did not respond to the suggestion, Southey took up the work himself and began to write in earnest in 1814 as a result of a conversation with Miss Mary Barker, Mrs Southey and Mrs Coleridge, a conversation described in the first chapter under the heading 'A Family Party at A Next Door Neighbour's.' In 1824 he described the work thus:

> Such a variety of ingredients I think never before entered into
> any book which had a thread of continuity running through it.
> I promise you there is as much sense as nonsense there. It is very
> much like a trifle, where you have whipt cream at the top,
> sweetmeats below, and a good solid foundation of cake well
> steeped in ratafia. You will find a liberal expenditure of long

hoarded stores, such as the reading of few men could supply; satire and speculation; truths, some of which might beseem the bench or the pulpit, and others that require the sanction of the cap and bells for their introduction. And withal a narrative interspersed with interludes of every kind; yet still continuous upon a plan of its own, varying from grave to gay; and taking as wild and yet as natural a course as one of our mountain streams (*Life*, vol. 5, p. 190).

Southey further described his sources:

I see in the work a little of Rabelais, but not much; more of Tristram Shandy, somewhat of Burton, and perhaps more of Montaigne; but methinks the *quintum quid* predominates (*Life*, vol. 6, p. 269).

The likeness to *Tristram Shandy* is most apparent in the rambling plot, but the really dominant element is the *quintum quid*, or rather Southey himself. The author-narrator is the principal character, much more so than is the titular hero, Dr Daniel Dove, as the narrator displays his widespread reading and his own thoughts upon a wide range of subjects.

Although the first two volumes of *The Doctor* were published anonymously and although John Lockhart in his review for the *Quarterly* did not penetrate the disguise, other readers did. H. C. Robinson said: 'I have no doubt, whatever, that it is by Southey' because the quotations from Spanish literature and old English 'odd citations' gave away the author's secret. The book contains Southey's likes and dislikes, but he restrains, on the whole, his strongest prejudices. The author shows himself to be a great lover of old books, old customs, and old ways of life. He is unconvinced that the changes in the social and economic structure have brought unmixed blessings. Even as Southey preferred for himself a life away from the bustle of a great city, so he depicts in the story of the Doves an idealized life of a family who had just enough material wealth to enable them to live respectably with education and leisure for some study and reading.

The plot of *The Doctor* is so slight as to be almost non-existent. We are introduced to a small group of persons and trace the life of the principal character, Dr Daniel Dove, from his birth in 1723 until his marriage. Other characters are his parents, Daniel and Dinah Dove, his uncle William Dove, who had a rich fund of traditional stories and proverbs, the schoolmaster Richard Guy, and Daniel's benefactor Peter Hopkins, who provided for his medical education at Leyden. The family of Daniel's wife consisted of her parents, Leonard and Deborah Bacon, and the author digressed to tell the story of their courtship and marriage. In addition to these two families, the author introduces neighbors of the Bacons, Mr Allison, a retired tobacconist from London, and his sister. Except for a few minor characters, briefly introduced, such as Mrs Bacon's beautiful and ill-tempered aunt, Millicent Trewbody, and Rowland Dixon and his puppets, *The Doctor* has fewer than a dozen characters.

Very little happens to this cast of characters. The hero, Daniel Dove, is educated at the school at Ingleton, which is conducted by the gentle Richard Guy, who encourages him in his studies. Daniel then studies medicine in Leyden, learns the Dutch language, falls in love with a Burgomeester's daughter whom he never meets, and returns to England, where he begins the practice of medicine at Doncaster. His introduction to his future wife, Deborah Bacon, occurred when her father brought his daughter, aged nineteen, to be inoculated for the smallpox because of an outbreak of that disease in the neighborhood. This meeting led to a friendship between the two men. The nearest thing to a complication in the plot occurs some time afterwards when a well-to-do and middle-aged neighbor, Mr Hebblethwaite, asks Mr Bacon for his daughter's hand in marriage. Mr Bacon would not force his daughter to marry against her wishes, and he is pleased when she refuses Mr Hebblethwaite with vehemence because, although she knows nothing evil concerning her suitor, she knows nothing good. But Mr Bacon had wished that his daughter be married since in the event of his own death he did not wish to leave her unprotected. He discussed this matter with Dr Dove who asked him:

'And you have made up your mind to part with her?'
'Upon a clear conviction that I ought to do so; that it is best for herself and me.'
'Well then, you will allow me to converse with her first, upon a different subject. You will permit me to see whether I can speak more successfully for myself, than you have done for Joseph Hebblethwaite. Have I your consent?'
Mr Bacon rose in great emotion, and taking his friend's hand pressed it fervently and tremulously. Presently they heard the wicket open, and Deborah came in.

'I dare say, Deborah,' said her father, composing himself, 'you have been telling Betsey Allison of the advantageous offer that you have this day refused.'

'Yes,' replied Deborah; 'and what do you think she said? That little as she liked him, rather than that I should be thrown away upon such a man, she could almost make up her mind to marry him herself.'

'And I,' said the Doctor, 'rather than such a man should have you would marry you myself.'

'Was not I right in refusing him, Doctor?'

'So right, that you never pleased me so well before; and never can please me better, – unless you will accept of me in his stead.'

She gave a little start, and looked at him half incredulously, and half angrily withal; as if what he had said was too light in its manner to be serious, and yet too serious in its import to be spoken in jest. But when he took her by the hand, and said, 'Will you, dear Deborah?' with a pressure, and in a tone that left no doubt of his earnest meaning, she cried, 'Father, what am I to say? speak for me!' – 'Take her, my friend!' said Mr Bacon; 'My blessing be upon you both. And if it be not presumptuous to use the words, – let me say for myself, "Lord, now lettest thou thy servant depart in peace!"'

And so does Southey describe the proposal of marriage and its acceptance between his hero and heroine.

The narrative method of *The Doctor* is digressive, and a part of the humor of the work consists in spinning out the story by telling one tale after another at the whim of the author. The result is rather like a series of essays upon miscellaneous topics or in some instances like materials gleaned from the author's *Common-Place Book*. Once Southey has introduced his characters and described their places of residence, he has abundant opportunity for introducing these topics. Mr Bacon, a clergyman, is described as an idealized parish priest, conscientious and reasonable in the performance of his duties and assiduous in seeing that the children of the parish are instructed in the Bible and good church doctrine. The description of the retired tobacconist, Mr Allison, gives not only the opportunity to describe his business in London, but to give the author's views of the place of the small shopkeeper in the economy. Southey strongly favored the individual who farms his own land, runs his own business, and achieves his own independence. The great combinations of capital in the form of large-scale agriculture and combinations of trade and manufacturing were threats to the old way of life. The description of the good life of the Bacons, the Doves, and the Allisons contained an implicit criticism of those economic changes that were altering the nature of English society. This nostalgia for a simpler style of life than that of the industrial-urban way has as perennial an appeal today as when Southey wrote over a century ago.

The autobiographical element in *The Doctor* is very strong. Not only do many chapters in the book reflect Southey's views on scores of subjects, but the characters William Dove and Millicent Trewbody are descriptions of his uncle William Tyler and his aunt Elizabeth Tyler. It is further a very personal work which he wrote *con amore* because he wished to write it and not because of any economic necessity. He took up the work at intervals over a period of thirty years, a fact that explains much of the discursive nature of the book.

Not everyone will care for *The Doctor*. It is a book best read in bits and pieces as a bedside book to be picked up and put down at pleasure rather than read consecutively for several hours. Henry Crabb Robinson thought the humor coarse, but Edgar Allan Poe admired its wit and humor. Lockhart liked least the attempts at humor and called his jocularity 'pedantic and chilling – his drollery wire-drawn, super-quaint, Whistlecraftish.' The book, however, will always have an honored place among literary classics because it contains within its covers – the fourth volume – that unquestioned classic of the nursery, the Story of the Three Bears. It should be noted that Southey's account has not the Goldilocks of the current version but a little old woman, and the story as Southey prints it distinguishes the various speakers by type appropriate to the size of the bears – Gothic, large capitals, and small italic.

The most attractive parts of *The Doctor* are the chapters describing the Doves, the Bacons, and the Allisons. To anyone who is a lover of cats, the delightful chapter on the Cats of Greta Hall will bring great pleasure. Less well known are the chapters on shaving (chapters 103–6), and the chapter on women (chapter 208) which quotes widely from anti-feminist literature, but whose seriousness may be gauged by the fanciful derivation of *mulier* which 'whatever grammarians may pretend, is plainly a comparative, applied exclusively and with peculiar force to denote the only creature in nature which is more mulish than mule.' The essay quality of *The Doctor* has already been stressed, and certain chapters or portions of them can be read as examples of the familiar essay, such as those on early friendships (chapter 47), on pockets (chapter 5), on Rowland Dixon and his puppets (chapter 22), and on schoolbooks, particularly the account of Textor's *Dialogues* (chapter 20).

If ever a work cried out for abridgment it is *The Doctor*. The original seven volumes are well printed and illustrated with a variety of types and with several colored illustrations, but the work is scarce, and M. H. FitzGerald's one-volume abridgment (about one-third of the whole) can be recommended as containing all that a reader may wish.

6

Histories

In sheer bulk Southey's histories loom as the largest and most formidable of any category in which he wrote. Both his *History of the Peninsular War* (1823–32) and his *History of Brazil* (1810–19) consisted of three large quartos of several hundred pages in each volume. His *Book of the Church* (1824) in two much smaller octavo volumes contained several hundred pages. It is doubtful that these volumes have many readers in this century, and the question arises whether anything there is worth saving, but any general assessment of Southey as a writer must consider these works.

The History of the Peninsular War

The History of the Peninsular War was an account not of an event in the past but one within the memory of all. Here Southey was describing the brave deeds of the Spanish and Portuguese peoples as they rose during the years from 1807 to 1813 to turn out, with the aid of their British allies under the future Duke of Wellington, the French invaders led by Napoleon. It was a fine story with a beginning, a middle, and a conclusion that could not fail to encourage every lover of freedom and of national independence. The war had been also a decisive factor in the ultimate defeat of the French. Southey's sources were the official dispatches of the day supplemented by a variety of pamphlets, diaries, and accounts of those who participated in the fight. His method was to record the events of the struggle in minute detail, but his tendency was to tell too much. Not content with describing the events as they took place, he paused to give a complete description of each town or village, some account of its history, its architecture, and any interesting legend or story attached to it. He also included a host of proclamations and documents in their entirety instead of briefly summarizing their contents.

Southey undertook the composition and publication of *The History of the Peninsular War* by agreement with John Murray for the sum of one thousand guineas. On June 10, 1812 he had written Scott of his interest in writing a history of the Spanish war, but it was not until about five years later that the matter was settled with Murray. Southey was by no means unfamiliar with the materials for this history, and indeed had already done a great deal of the writing and the research during his composition of the 'History of the Year' for the years 1808 through 1811 for the first four volumes of the *Edinburgh Annual Register*. Southey did not hide the fact that he could use much of the material in the *Register* for the new history, but he was silent as to the extent of that use. A comparison of the *Register* and the *Peninsular War* shows that Southey was able to use about 30 per cent of what he had published in the *Register* in the history.* It is only fair to state that Southey often revised the material from the *Register* and that most of the history has information which he gained from sources not available to him at the time he wrote the *Register*. He was unfortunate, however, in not having access to the Duke of Wellington's materials, and it was here that Sir William Napier had the advantage of him.

Southey's *Peninsular War* has not stood up well in a comparison with General Sir William Napier's six-volume *History of the War in the Peninsula and the South of France* (1828–40). Napier's and not Southey's has become the authoritative work upon the war. Southey in his history too often loses himself in antiquarian and historical detail and fails to understand the principles of military tactics and strategy. Napier does not fall into this error of judgment. Southey's hatred of Napoleon and of the French also leads him into a view of the struggle as something like a holy war in which the Spaniards rose up as one man to expel the invader. As a consequence Southey does not give sufficient credit to the crucial part played by the British forces and Wellington in the series of battles which effected the final defeat of the French forces. Napier, on the other hand, had been personally involved in some of the engagements and understood professionally military tactics and strategy. Wellington himself was not impressed by Southey's work and is reported by Samuel Rogers as having said 'I

---

* It would be tedious to give a minute listing of these borrowings, but chapters 12–23, minus 17, from the *Register* for 1808 are largely identical with chapters 2–5, 8–9, 11–12 of the first volume of the *Peninsular War*. Lesser passages of correspondence will be found between the other three volumes of the *Register* and the other two of the *Peninsular War*.

don't think much of it' (*Recollections of the Table-Talk of Samuel Rogers*, 1856, p. 289).

Despite the shortcomings of Southey's history there are still good things within the volumes. The narrative is well told, and if the author is too often diverted by his fondness for inserting irrelevant historical detail and anecdote, he is still effective when describing stories of individual heroism. An excerpt from the history which received praise is his account of the siege of Zaragoza (chapter IX). The valor of the Maid of Zaragoza became a legend in its own day. Here is Southey's description:

> The carnage here [before the gate Portillo] throughout the day was dreadful. Augustina Zaragoza, a handsome woman of the lower class, about twenty-two years of age, arrived at this battery with refreshments, at the time when not a man who defended it was left alive, so tremendous was the fire which the French kept up against it. For a moment the citizens hesitated to re-man the guns. Augustina sprung forward over the dead and dying, snatched a match from the hand of a dead artilleryman, and fired off a six-and-twenty pounder; then, jumping upon the gun, made a solemn vow never to quit it alive during the siege. Such a sight could not but animate with fresh courage all who beheld it. The Zaragozans rushed into the battery, and renewed their fire with greater vigour than ever, and the French were repulsed here, and at all other points, with great slaughter.

And Southey's comment on the success of the effort of the Zaragozans:

> There is not, either in the annals of ancient or of modern times, a single event recorded more worthy to be held in admiration, now and for evermore, than the siege of Zaragoza. . . . They performed their duty; they redeemed their souls from the yoke; they left an example to their country, never to be forgotten, never to be out of mind, and sure to contribute to and hasten its deliverance.

The History of Brazil

The great unwritten opus of Southey's career was his History of Portugal. He planned this work at the age of twenty-six during his second trip to Portugal, with the assistance of his uncle, the Reverend

Herbert Hill, and of Mr Hill's excellent collection of books and manuscripts. During that winter Southey began in earnest the research and study for that history which he never had time or leisure to complete. *The History of Brazil* is, however, a result of that interest and contains some of the materials he had collected for the history of the mother country. The designs of Napoleon upon the Iberian peninsula turned the eyes of Europe towards Spain and Portugal, and when in 1807 the Portuguese royal family sailed for refuge to Brazil, public attention was drawn to the colony. British interest became lively in that sector when a commercial treaty was signed that gave the British concessions and opened the Brazilian ports to foreign ships. With attention thus drawn towards Portugal and especially to Brazil, Southey decided to write the history of the colony. *The History of Brazil* appeared in three large quarto volumes in 1810, 1817, and 1819.

Although the size of these volumes may intimidate, the reader interested in any aspect of Brazilian history from its founding in 1500 until the year 1808 has before him all the information he could possibly want. Southey's research, care, and industry were enormous. The method of narration was chronological with the dates inserted in the margins, and he was always careful to indicate the sources of his information. Sir Walter Scott found the events absorbing. 'I have traced the achievements of the Portuguese adventurers with greater interest than I remember to have felt since, when a school-boy, I first perused the duodecimo collection of Voyages and Discoveries called the World Displayed' (*Letters of Scott*, vol. 2, p. 341).

But it is feared that most readers did not find *The History of Brazil* quite so absorbing as did Scott. Southey confessed that the sale of the history had netted him less than one article in the *Quarterly* so that the sale must have been disappointing despite the fact that the first volume went into a second edition in 1822. The subject of the history was of little interest to most English-speaking readers, however much public attention may have been diverted to matters Spanish and Portuguese during the years of the Peninsular War. Certainly their interest was not sufficient to make very many readers want to read three huge quartos. Southey made the common mistake that a specialist is prone to make in assuming that everyone else is as much interested in his subject as he is himself. He believed that any and every fact concerning Brazilian history and topography should be set down, and he failed too often to indicate the significance of these facts. Reginald Heber in his review of the first volume in the *Quarterly* complained of this 'want of broad and general views of his subject, and of those bird's eye recapitulations, which serve as a resting-place to the attention, and bring at once before the reader's observation the relative harmony of the objects he has gone through in detail' (*Quarterly Review*, vol. 4, p. 472).

The History of Brazil has, however, been treasured by the Brazilians, translated into Portuguese, and is still the best in English for colonial Brazil, but F. A. Varnhagen's *Historia general do Brasil* (1877) has superseded Southey's work.

A reader who wishes to sample this history would do well to turn to Southey's account of the Jesuit Reductions in the second volume (pp. 333–56), a selection reprinted by Jacob Zeitlin in his anthology of Southey's prose. The Jesuits had organized a benevolent social system for the government of the Indians designed to lead them into a civilized and Christian way of life and to protect them from the barbaric ways of their neighbors. A thoroughly paternalistic society, it is none the less – as related by Southey – a charming idyll of an ordered existence within the disorder of savage life and the sometimes equally savage and cruel practices of the European colonialists.

The Book of the Church

The Book of the Church, published in 1824, enjoyed something of a popular success and went into several editions, a seventh edition in 1859 and a later reprint in the Chandos Library. Henry Crabb Robinson recorded in his diary for March 16, 1824:

> I . . . read Southey's *Book of the Church*, which has been my great amusement since. A very entertaining book, even though it succeeded the *Arabian Nights*. The narrative of the conflict between Becket and Henry II is related with the spirit of a novel and the detail of the persecutions under Henry VIII and Queen Mary is only too uniformly horrid for tragedy, and I have not yet met with anything to object to; but I am now beginning his account of the Puritans, in which I shall probably find exceptionable matter (*Henry Crabb Robinson on Books and Their Writers*, 1938, vol. I, p. 303).

Lord Radnor's pleasure in *The Book of the Church* led him to his decision to offer Southey a seat in Parliament.

The Book of the Church is not simply a popular history of the Church of England, but was a part of the public debate over the question of

Catholic Emancipation. Southey's determined and bitter opposition to the Roman Church finds full expression in his book, and the topicality of this point of view lessens the pleasure for many modern readers. In his account of the Church during the Middle Ages, Southey stresses the struggle between Popes and Kings and the deception and dishonesty of the Papacy. He also tells many tales of fraud and deceit in connection with relics and in the dissemination of miraculous stories concerning the lives of the saints. When he reaches the sixteenth century full scope is given to the harshness with which each side persecuted its opponents. A reader today may not relish these accounts of burnings at the stake in the name of religion.

But there are passages in *The Book of the Church* that will reinforce Robinson's judgment. Robinson, incidentally, was a Unitarian and not sympathetic to most of Southey's positions about the Church, education, and Catholic emancipation. Southey's great skill as a writer of prose is his ability at narration and his judicious use of quotation from his authorities. He may, it is true, be a little lengthy, but he always rises to the occasion when he must describe one of the famous events in history. Robinson is quite right in selecting the famous confrontation between Henry II and Becket for praise. Southey is best when his sympathies are with his subject. So his description of the Lollards and John Wyclif and of the early attempts to translate the Bible are also outstanding. When he comes to the terrible days of the reigns of Henry VIII and Queen Mary he is on the whole very effective in narrating these events. His sympathy for Sir Thomas More comes out clearly, and he also says what can be said on behalf of Henry – unlike those modern historians who find little to praise. His accounts of the martyrdoms of Bishops Latimer and Ridley are vividly told, and his account of Archbishop Cranmer – of his character and his death at the stake – is movingly and ably narrated.

When Southey comes to the religious controversies of the seventeenth century he sides with the Church against the Puritans and is the partisan of Archbishop Laud. His history ends with the reign of James II. A few sentences from the past page of his work will indicate something of his purpose in writing the book:

> From the time of the Revolution the Church of England has
> partaken of the stability and security of the State. Here
> therefore I terminate this compendious, but faithful, view of its
> rise, progress, and political struggles. It has rescued us, first from

heathenism, then from papal idolatry and superstition; it has saved us from temporal as well as spiritual despotism. We owe to it our moral and intellectual character as a nation; much of our private happiness, much of our public strength. Whatever should weaken it, would in the same degree injure the common weal; whatever should overthrow it, would in sure and immediate consequence bring down the goodly fabric of that Constitution, whereof it is a constituent and necessary part.

The Church of England is therefore an essential part of the State and whatever weakens the Church weakens the State. Coleridge's *Constitution of Church and State* is a work with a different emphasis, but both books share much of the same point of view. A poetical parallel is Wordsworth's series of Ecclesiastical Sonnets, a record in verse of the history of the Church of England. Southey's work needs, therefore, to be read in light of the controversies and interests of its age rather than as a history isolated from the time in which it was written.

What can a reader of today find in *The Book of the Church*? It is doubtful that many would wish to read the work completely, but Robinson's comment is true that in parts it reads with the force of a novel, and the reader would be recommended to read chapters 8 and 9 of the account of Henry and Becket and especially Henry's penance at the shrine; chapter 12, the reign of Henry VIII; chapter 14, the reign of Mary; the account of Laud in chapter 17. As narratives these passages are vigorously written. If they dwell a little too much upon martyrdom, they also contain an absorbing human interest and stress the heroic qualities of those who gave their lives on behalf of the Church.

7

Reviews, Editions, and Translations

Reviews

Southey devoted a large part of his working life to reviewing. His first reviews were for the *Critical Review* (1797–8) and were, on the whole, rather perfunctory. His more substantial reviews were for the *Annual Review* (1802–9) and the *Quarterly Review* (1809–39) with occasional reviews for the *Foreign Review* (1828–30) and the *Foreign Quarterly Review* (1827). It can be argued that the task work was not really burdensome. The pay from the *Quarterly* was generous, and he often received as much for one article as from the royalties of a book. The *Quarterly*, moreover, reached a wide audience. By virtue of being a reviewer Southey received a steady supply of books and pamphlets; he was forced, as a consequence, to read, write, and think about a great many topics that he would have left untouched had he been left to his own pursuits. Despite the anonymity of reviewing in those days – and the misattribution of articles to him – Southey's work for the *Quarterly* contributed greatly to his own reputation. As Gifford said: 'Southey's prose is so good that every one detects him' (S. Smiles, *A Publisher and His Friends*, 1891, vol. 1, p. 260). As Gifford also generously admitted, Southey's reviews contributed significantly to the prosperity of the *Review*. The reviews, furthermore, led both directly and indirectly to the publication of books. Southey's review of some biographies of Nelson for the *Quarterly* led to Murray's commission of the famous *Life of Nelson*. Southey's review of Myles's *History of the Methodists* in the *Annual Review* (1803) contained an outline of Wesley's life and is the germ of his biography of Wesley (1820). The topics which he discussed in the reviews on social and political conditions are echoed and paralleled in his *Colloquies on the Progress and Prospects of Society* (1829).

During the seven-year life of the *Annual Review* (1802–9) Southey wrote over 150 reviews for that periodical, ranging from a notice of one paragraph to a six- or seven-page review article on the subject suggested by the book. Edited by Arthur Aikin and published by Longman, the *Annual* attempted to comment upon almost every book published during the preceding year. Southey once described his method of reviewing in the following words:

> I believe myself to be a good reviewer in my own way, which is that of giving a succinct account of the contents of the book before me, extracting its essence, bringing my own knowledge to bear upon the subject, and, where occasion serves, seasoning it with those opinions which in some degree leaven all my thoughts, words, and actions.

Most of the reviews in the *Annual* pretty much follow this pattern. In so far as he could, Southey let the author tell his own story by giving extensive quotations. This method worked especially well for books of travel, to which he usually devoted his longest articles. In this category his reviews of Bruce's *Travels to Discover the Source of the Nile* and of John Barrow's *Africa* and *Voyage to Cochin-China* deserve mention. Although Southey's specialty in reviewing was never belles-lettres, he did review the works of such contemporaries as W. S. Landor, Thomas Moore, and W. L. Bowles and editions or biographies of older writers: Todd's Spenser, Zouch's Sidney, Godwin's Chaucer, Ellis's *Specimens* and Scott's edition of *Sir Tristrem*. His liveliest and most trenchant articles are on general topics. The *Report* of the Society for the Suppression of Vice received the full force of his vituperative scorn. The society, employing informers to further its works, had as its principal object the prosecution of small shopkeepers and publicans who sold their goods and services to the poor on Sunday, which was the only day, Southey pointed out, many of the poor could shop. Southey's review of Malthus's *Essay on the Principle of Population* (vol. 2, pp. 292–301) is a spirited attack upon the measures recommended by Malthus since they appealed to the rich and hard-hearted:

> This reformer calls for no sacrifice from the rich; on the contrary, he proposes to relieve them from their parish rates; he recommends nothing to them but that they should harden their hearts. They have found a place at the table of nature; and why should they be disturbed at their feast? It is Mr. Malthus's own metaphor!

Southey's conclusion is a quotable one: 'He writes advice to the poor for the rich to read.'

One of the most thoughtful of Southey's reviews for the *Annual* was his review of William Myles's *History of the Methodists*. The review gives a succinct account of Wesley's life, the growth and organization of the Methodist societies, and a warning of the danger which the Methodists pose to the established Church. Southey objects to their practice of group confession and to their sermons 'seasoned with brimstone, and glowing with fire.' By 1820 Southey in his biography of Wesley modified some of his views and hoped for the ultimate return of the Methodists to the Church of England. Southey's attitude towards the Church – not to be confused with his own doctrinal beliefs – seems to have been consistent. Although he was not uncritical of its shortcomings, he stressed its tendency to ignore its responsibilities and possibilities in the fields of education and of missions. His review of the account of the Baptist Mission in India (vol. 1, pp. 207–18) praised the zeal of William Carey and his associates, their translation of the scriptures into Bengalee, and urged the Established Church to sponsor a missionary society. Southey recommended that individuals encourage what the Baptists had started since the introduction of Christianity into India could be a means of rooting out polygamy, human sacrifices, infanticide, and self-torture. Southey's first article in the *Quarterly* was likewise a review of the work of this same group of Baptist missionaries, who had during the interim earned the scorn of Sydney Smith in the *Edinburgh Review*.

Of the several hundred books published during the days of the *Annual Review* very few are remembered today. In 1806, after three years of reviewing for the *Annual*, Southey indicated that the reviews of the Baptist Mission, of Malthus, of Myles's history, and of the Society for the Suppression of Vice indicated the state of his opinions (*Life*, vol. 3, pp. 21–2). Books of historical importance appeared, and Southey was quick to recognize the importance and literary value of one in particular: *The Memoirs of the Life of Colonel Hutchinson* written by his widow Lucy and edited by one of his descendants for the first time in 1806.* Southey's review of this memoir is a highly readable biographical essay of an important person – he was one of the regicides who signed the Charles I's death-warrant – during the Cromwellian era (vol. 5, pp. 361–7). Southey's coadjutors in the *Annual Review* were

---

* A. W. Ward praises the work highly in the *Cambridge History of English Literature*, vol. 7, pp. 225–7.

William Taylor of Norwich, Arthur and Lucy Aikin, their aunt, Mrs Anna L. Barbauld, together with several Unitarian ministers. Southey declared, with more truth than modesty, that 'if William Taylor and I were to forsake it, Mr. Longman might as well think of living without his liver and lungs, as of keeping his Review alive without us' (*Letters*, vol. 1, p. 282). The competition of the newly founded *Quarterly* in 1809 and the departure of Southey made the continuation of the *Annual* a doubtful speculation, and its last volume in 1809 had only two reviews by Southey.

Southey's most important reviewing was for the *Quarterly Review* to which he contributed almost a hundred articles. These reviews followed a pattern already established by the reviewers of the *Edinburgh Review* and by Southey himself in some of his reviewing for the *Annual*. This method was to take a book (or books) as a text and then write an independent essay that often only cursorily glanced at the books ostensibly under review. Extensive quotation from the work was sometimes a feature, especially for books of poetry and of travel.

William Gifford, the editor and a friend of Grosvenor Bedford, had approached Southey to be a contributor, and Southey had agreed, stating that he felt especially able to deal with history, biography, and travel. From the editor's point of view Southey was an ideal contributor since he could always be counted upon for an able article punctually submitted to meet the deadline for the next issue. Southey, however, constantly chafed under what he regarded as Gifford's mutilation of his articles; the editor often omitted passages or toned down statements to make them fit the position of the *Review*.

A full discussion of Southey's *Quarterly* contributions could easily fill a volume, but a quick survey of the categories and books he noticed will give a clear idea of their scope and contents.* Although Southey was suspected of having written reviews of the famous poems of Shelley and Hunt, he actually reviewed very few works of his contemporary poets. Landor's *Count Julian* is the best known of the poems he did review. This poem together with poems by James Grahame, James Montgomery, and the obscure poetesses Lucretia Davidson and Mary Colling make up the list. He reviewed the collected works of William Hayley and Frank Sayers, but he never reviewed the poems of what

---

* The most complete account of Southey's *Quarterly* articles with special discussion of separate articles is by Geoffrey Carnall, *Robert Southey and His Age*.

today are considered the major poets. Other articles on literary topics are an article on Portuguese literature, an essay on Camoens, and a review of Lord Holland's translation of Lope de Vega. His most ambitious literary review was his two-part review of Alexander Chalmers's *English Poets*.

The reviewing of travel books was a specialty of Southey as he noticed books of travel from Polynesia to Iceland. He was especially interested in the accounts of the United States and reviewed the Lewis and Clarke expedition, Abiel Holmes's *American Annals*, and Timothy Dwight's *Travels in New England and New York*. These reviews gave him an opportunity to redress the anti-American stance of the *Quarterly*, about which he protested in vain to Murray and Gifford. Occasionally, Southey was able to bring into favorable notice the work of a friend: the reviews of James Burney's *History of the Voyages and Discoveries in the South Sea*, Henry Koster's *Travels in Brazil*, and his brother Thomas Southey's *Chronological History of the West Indies*.*

The most skilful and interesting group of *Quarterly* articles are the short biographies which Southey wrote as ostensible reviews of a book or memoir. These have been already discussed in the section on biography: lives of Nelson, Wellington, Marlborough, Cromwell, Bayard – all military leaders; John Evelyn, William Huntington, John Oberlin, and Thomas Telford.

The fourth group of articles by Southey on social, political, and general topics is difficult to discuss because of the varied nature of the material. The points of view expressed in these articles are more interestingly given in the Espriella letters and in the *Colloquies*. The articles in the *Quarterly* can often be read as part of the *Quarterly's* – and of Southey's own – continuing quarrel with the *Edinburgh Review*. His views of the missionaries (1809), on education in the Bell and Lancaster controversy, on Catholic Emancipation, and on the conduct of the war in Spain were all in direct opposition to the positions of the rival quarterly. Southey's fear of a civil war, although happily unrealized, was genuine, and the frequent outbursts of rioting and violence

* A difficulty in discussing Southey's *Quarterly* articles is that no exact list has ever been compiled. Cuthbert Southey's list (*Life*, vol. 6, pp. 400–2) is demonstrably inaccurate and has led to confusion. The reviews of John Anderson's *Sumatra* (1826), Head's *Rough Notes* and Miers's *Chile* (1827), and Sparks's *John Ledyard* (1828), although on Cuthbert's list, are clearly not by Southey. The same list, however, fails to include the review of Pasley (1811), which is partly by Southey, and the article on the Corn Laws (1834), which he claimed as his.

made him apprehensive as to the future. He felt that concessions to the Roman Catholics and changes in the way that Parliament was selected could only exacerbate the situation. At the same time he was, as every reader of Espriella and the *Colloquies* was aware, eager for every sort of humanitarian reform and for the active role of the government in promoting changes. His articles on the poor, the poor laws, and the means of improving the people (1812, 1816, 1818) are illustrative of his concern. All these articles he chose to reprint in 1832 in his *Essays*. The issues about which Southey wrote were of vital concern in his day and were resolved during his own and the next generation. Although the same questions often arise in the twentieth century, the discussions in the *Quarterly* will today chiefly interest the reader with an historical bent.

Editions and Translations

A minor portion of Southey's literary achievement was in the realm of editing and translating. Publishers believed that his name upon the title-page would ensure the sale of the edition. Although Southey took pains in the preparation of these editions, his standards are hardly those of twentieth-century scholarship, and his editorial labors have been superseded by more authoritative editions. His edition of Malory's *Morte D'Arthur* (1817), a reprint of the text of Caxton's first edition, was published by Longman in two quarto volumes. Handsomely printed with woodcuts and large readable type, this edition had an important role in the nineteenth-century revival of interest in Malory. It was through Southey's edition that Pre-Raphaelites such as Burne-Jones, Morris, and Rossetti knew the *Morte D'Arthur* (B. Gaines, 'The Editions of Malory in the Early Nineteenth Century,' *Publications of the Bibliographical Society of America*, 68, 1974, pp. 1–17). Southey's *Select Works of the British Poets, From Chaucer to Jonson* (1831) is a stout octavo volume of over one thousand pages containing copious selections of the works of poets from Chaucer through Lovelace including the complete *Faerie Queene*. No poems of Shakespeare, however, are included, and Ben Jonson is completely omitted despite the promise of the title page. The biographical introductions are short with very little analysis of the poems. A moral note is a constant theme: authors such as Daniel and Carew are praised for their commendable personal qualities. A comment on Davenant's and Dryden's version of *The Tempest* is quotable:

His last work was his worst; it was an alteration of the Tempest, executed in conjunction with Dryden; and marvellous indeed it is that two men of such great and indubitable genius should have combined to debase, and vulgarise, and pollute such a poem as the Tempest: but, to the scandal of the English stage, it is their Tempest, and not Shakespeare's, which is to this day represented (p. 913).

Southey's *Specimens of the Later English Poets* (1807), originally designed as supplementary to Ellis's *Specimens*, was an unsatisfactory collaboration with Grosvenor Bedford, and deserves the censure it has received (by R. D. Havens, *PMLA*, vol. 60, 1945).

Several of Southey's editorial tasks were undertaken to help authors or their families. The first such task was his collaboration with Joseph Cottle in producing his three-volume edition of the works of Thomas Chatterton (1803), the proceeds of which went to Chatterton's mother and sister. His edition and short biographical essay on Henry Kirke White was a memorial to a poet who had died young and whose poems deserved preservation. In 1831 he edited *Attempts in Verse*, written by John Jones, an old servant, to which he added brief biographical sketches of several uneducated poets, an essay which J. S. Childers reprinted (1925) as *The Lives and Works of the Uneducated Poets*. An edition of Bunyan (1830), of Isaac Watts's *Horae Lyricae* (1834), and of William Cowper (1835–7) completed his editorial labors.

Southey's knowledge of the Spanish and Portuguese languages and literatures made him an ideal translator and editor of the works of authors from these countries. His three most important translations are his *Amadis of Gaul* (4 vols, 1803), *Palmerin of England* (4 vols, 1807) and his *Chronicle of the Cid* (1808). The translations of *Amadis* and of the *Cid* are original, but that of *Palmerin* is a correction and revision of Anthony Munday's translation of 1588. The archaic flavor of the translation is an objection sometimes made to Southey's translations, but his attempt to give the impression of a work written in medieval times by archaizing the language is certainly defensible and a practice of many translators since Southey's day. All these translations of Southey have been reprinted several times since their original publication; an especially handsome reprint of his *Cid* appeared in 1958 by the Limited Editions Club with an appreciative essay by V. S. Pritchett.

During the years of his laureateship to the *Morning Post*, Southey translated many short poems not only from Spanish and Portuguese but also from French, Italian, Latin, and Greek. These translations lie for the most part uncollected and unclaimed within the files of that newspaper, but many are scattered throughout his *Common-Place Book* and in his letters. Southey occasionally included his own translations in his reviews, in a series of letters on the Spanish poets in the *Monthly Magazine* (1797-9), and he once planned to publish a volume of his translations of Camoens' short poems.

Part **III**

Poetry

8

Early Poems, *Joan of Arc*, and Short Poems

Southey made his literary reputation as a poet, and he wrote most of his poetry between 1794 and 1814 – between his twentieth and fortieth years. Both his facility and range are amazing: there is almost no form to which he did not turn his hand, and the body of his poetry contains a comprehensive view of the poetic interests of his age. After his first volume of poems (1795) – published jointly with Robert Lovell – Southey can be seen to be working in the forms that were coming into fashion, and also helping to form the fashion and the taste of the age. His first volume can be passed over quickly – 'The Retrospect' was the only poem he chose to reprint – with the statement that it shows principally that the writer had been a close reader of such eighteenth-century poets as Gray, Collins, the Wartons, Sayers, Bowles, and Cowper and was attracted to such forms as the sonnet, short poems in blank verse, and unrhymed odes.

Southey's first ambitious work – and his first success – came in 1796 with the publication of *Joan of Arc*, a handsomely published quarto, full of new revolutionary ideas from Rousseau, Godwin, and the French Revolution, but written in the epic style with many a reminiscence of Milton in the form of epic simile and inverted word order. Southey had been working on *Joan* since his Oxford days in 1793 and the poem underwent much revision before it saw the light of day. The plot of *Joan of Arc* is very simple. Joan, who has been roused by visions, is made aware of the plight of France and the horrors of war produced by the English invaders, and resolves to save her country. She goes to the King, convinces him, leads an army which succeeds in raising the siege at Orleans, and witnesses the triumph of Charles as he is crowned at Rheims. The subsequent career of Joan, so familiar to readers of later versions of her story, is not part of the work. The heroine of Southey's poem is a leader of her country in a holy war of liberty and national independence against an invader. Her education – supplied by Southey – had been Rousseauistic, and her natural innocence had never been corrupted by society. She is ever mindful of the blessings of a simple life, of the sad fate of the many victims of oppression and war, seeks no vengeance upon the soldiers of the enemy, her wrath being reserved for kings, tyrants, courtiers, the oppressors of mankind. The parallels with the situation between France and England in the 1790s were very evident, and the choice of a French heroine for an epic poem by an English poet could not but be noticed when English forces were arraigned against the French. Joan is thus not so much a re-creation of an historical figure as a symbol of the new ideals of liberty and equality, ideals that know no national boundaries. Her characterization is pretty flat, and she is less interesting than Conrade, whose vigorous action and final death in battle engage the reader's attention and interest. The work – however creditable for a young man of twenty – reveals a great want of technique. The long speeches are full of preaching as Joan talks or argues with friends, priests, or kings. When Southey is forced to describe battles, his notes (very extensive) show only too clearly that the passages are versified descriptions of such works as Grose's *Military Antiquities* with their accounts of medieval armor and the various engines of war used in sieges. Joan of Arc has a kinship with other leading characters in Southey's poems – such as Thalaba and Roderick, for she is one whose life is dedicated to a mission – she is in every sense the Maid of Destiny.

The reviewers were very kind to this poem. John Aikin in the *Monthly Review*, after pointing out blemishes and censuring the poet for his remarks in the preface about running a race with the press in getting *Joan* printed, declared 'That the poetical powers displayed . . . are of a very superior kind and . . . promise a rich harvest of future excellence,' while the anonymous reviewer in the *Critical Review* declared 'The poetical powers of Mr. Southey are indisputably very superior, and capable, we doubt not, of producing a poem that will place him in the first class of English poets' (*Robert Southey: The Critical Heritage*, ed. Lionel Madden, 1972, pp. 41, 45). Privately, others spoke out in praise. Charles Lamb's letter to Coleridge (ibid, pp. 45, 46) was extravagantly enthusiastic. 'Why the poem is alone sufficient to redeem the character of the age we live in from the imputation of degenerating in Poetry. . . . On the whole I expect Southey one day to rival Milton.' Southey was well launched on his poetic career, and for those who were interested in literature, his was a name to watch.

After *Joan* Southey conceived the idea of writing another long narrative poem, this time upon the legendary Welsh hero Madoc, but after commencing the poem he put it aside for several years and turned to a Mohammedan hero, Thalaba, for his next subject. In the meantime, however, Southey devoted most of his poetic energies from 1796 through 1800 to short poems. Here the harvest was truly great. The forms and subjects were varied, and a brief look at their classification is instructive. Sonnets, ballads, and short tales in blank verse abound, and these are varied by epitaphs, inscriptions, eclogues, odes in unrhymed stanzas, as well as translations, chiefly from Spanish and Portuguese, but also from Italian, Latin, and French. The subjects are often simple stories of domestic life, and tales from history from all periods from Greece and Rome, including English kings and heroes, down to contemporary France. The most significant group of short poems is the grotesque ballad. Other poets dealt with other topics more successfully than Southey, but here he found a type of poetry suited to his talent and temperament. The grotesque ballad is usually based upon an incident from an old chronicle, it often deals with the supernatural, and it treats in a humorous fashion a story which handled otherwise would have been revolting or horrible as in the instance of Bishop Hatto, who is consumed by rats.

Southey's six months in Spain and Portugal in 1796 right after the publication of *Joan* gave him a breathing spell from too much writing, but the new scenes and the acquisition of two new languages supplied him with new topics and suggested the possibilities of translation. His *Letters Written During a Short Residence in Spain and Portugal* contain many translations of poetry. The year 1797 saw the publication of his *Poems* (a second edition was required during the year). Ideologically, the volume represents Southey's humanitarian interests, for here we find a group of poems on the African slave trade, the Botany Bay Eclogues, a series depicting the sad plight of those transported to that penal colony in Australia, and such poems (the content and tone can be inferred from their titles) as 'The Pauper's Funeral,' 'The Soldier's Wife,' 'The Widow,' and an inscription upon the regicide Henry Marten. Before the year 1797 was out Southey had agreed to supply Daniel Stuart, editor of the *Morning Post*, with verses at the rate of a guinea a week. Coleridge was already a contributor, Wordsworth had been published there, as well as a host of now forgotten poets such as Mrs Mary 'Perdita' Robinson and W. C. 'Clio' Rickman. This assignment Southey undertook with zeal so that scarcely a week passed without at least one poem from his pen. Here appeared some of his best as well as most anthologized pieces: 'The Battle of Blenheim,' 'The Holly Tree,' 'The Well of St. Keyne' and 'God's Judgement on a Wicked Bishop.' Southey was not one to let his pieces remain – although many did so – unclaimed and unreprinted in the files of a newspaper, and his *Annual Anthology* in 1799 and 1800, a miscellaneous collection of poetry largely written by Southey and his circle of fellow-poets, reprinted many of these poems. A second gathering from this same source came in 1805 with the three-volume collection of his minor poems, *Metrical Tales*.

The number and variety of poems which Southey wrote during these years is so great that it becomes difficult to select groups by form and subject matter for discussion, but some categories are prominent. The sonnet enjoyed during the latter part of the eighteenth century a revival that was to have a remarkable vitality. The five hundred or so sonnets of Wordsworth and the remarkable sonnets of Keats stand out as the finest contributions of Southey's contemporaries, but every poet tried his hand at a few. William Lisle Bowles appears to have been the catalyst for Southey and Coleridge. His *Fourteen Sonnets, Elegiac and Descriptive written during a tour* (Bath 1789) so appealed to both Southey and Coleridge that they copied these sonnets to share them with their friends. Today the sonnets seem the tamest of tame descriptions of peaceful rural scenes, but they did not so impress young poets looking for models, and Southey's 'With many a weary step, at length I gain/Thy summit, Lansdown' and 'To the Evening Rainbow' are written in that vein. A few lines from 'To the Evening Rainbow' will illustrate.

> Mild arch of promise, on the evening sky
> Thou shinest fair with many a lovely ray
> Each in the other melting. Much mine eye
> Delights to linger on thee; for the day,
> Changeful and many-weather'd, seem'd to smile
> Flashing brief splendour through the clouds awhile,
> Which deepen'd dark anon and fell in rain.

Other sonnets continue the Bowles-nature tradition with sonnets upon the lark, spring, the sun, the sturdy oak, but other themes are also introduced. Following the example of Milton, Southey used the sonnet for epistolary purposes, and his sonnet 'Fair be thy fortunes in the distant land' is a farewell to his Old Westminster friend George

Strachey as he left for India. Two very fine sonnets – in differing styles –
are the one on winter and the one addressed to a goose. The personified
picture of winter contains vivid and striking details, and contrasts the
harsh and genial sides of that season.

A Wrinkled, crabbed man they picture thee,
Old Winter, with a rugged beard as grey
As the long moss upon the apple-tree;
Blue-lipt, an ice-drop at thy sharp blue nose,
Close muffled up, and on thy dreary way,
Plodding alone through sleet and drifting snows.
They should have drawn thee by the high-heapt hearth,
Old Winter! seated in thy great arm'd chair,
Watching the children at their Christmas mirth;
Or circled by them as thy lips declare
Some merry jest or tale of murder dire,
Or troubled spirit that disturbs the night,
Pausing at times to rouse the mouldering fire,
Or taste the old October brown and bright.

Southey used the sonnet on several occasions for a light and humorous effect. 'To a Goose' is perhaps the best, and not so well known as it
deserves to be.

To a Goose
If thou didst feed on western plains of yore;
Or waddle wide with flat and flabby feet
Over some Cambrian mountain's plashy moor;
Or find in farmer's yard a safe retreat
From gipsy thieves, and foxes sly and fleet;
If thy grey quills, by lawyer guided trace
Deeds big with ruin to some wretched race,
Or love-sick poet's sonnet, sad and sweet,
Wailing the rigour of his lady fair;
Or if, the drudge of housemaid's daily toil,
Cobwebs and dust thy pinions white besoil,
Departed Goose! I neither know nor care.
But this I know, that we pronounced thee fine,
Season'd with sage and onions, and port wine.

The one sonnet pattern that he avoided was the Petrarchan love sonnet,
but he wrote instead parodies of the affected love sonnets of the Della

Cruscan school of Robert Merry and his associates under the heading of 'Love Elegies of Abel Shufflebottom.' The sonnets just quoted show at a glance several of Southey's poetic mannerisms – some of which received censure. The use of 'mine' for 'my' in the phrase 'mine eye'; the fondness for compounds, of his own devising, such as 'many-weather'd'; his addiction to alliteration, conveniently seen in 'waddle wide with flat and flabby feet'; and all-too-frequent indulgence in an inverted word order as 'foxes sly and fleet' and in the line 'Cobwebs and dust thy pinions white besoil.' The form of the sonnet, too, is generally irregular in its rhyme scheme. 'To a Goose' conforms neither to the textbook definition of the Italian nor to the Shakespearean model, but goes its own way. An inspection of other sonnets by Southey reveals the same indifference. Wordsworth and Keats – the masters of the sonnet from among Southey's contemporaries – were more careful in this matter.

Despite the interest in the sonnet and Southey's often successful handling of that ever-popular form, pride of place, in quality as well as in number, must be accorded to the group which he called Ballads and Metrical Tales. Many of these were based on stories Southey derived from his extensive reading in old black letter chronicles, while still others he composed from current stories that came to his attention. The most successful were those derived from old legends, written either in the simple ballad stanza (or a modification of that stanza), and the treatment accorded them was characteristically Southeyan: instead of dwelling upon the horror or the tragedy often implicit in the legend he chose rather to give it a humorous twist and to treat the manifestations of the supernatural with ironic and detached amusement.

This grotesque treatment is best illustrated in the following. 'The Old Woman of Berkeley,' who has devoted her life to witchcraft, hopes through the aid of the Church and her son and daughter – a monk and nun respectively – to avoid having to pay the consequences of an ill-spent life. But despite all that the Church can do, the devil comes at last and bears her away. 'The Inchcape Rock,' based upon an account in Stoddart's *Remarks on Scotland*, is a well-told narrative of the biter bit, as Ralph the Rover, having for his own nefarious purposes removed the warning bell from the Rock, comes to his own well-deserved end by shipwreck. The tone throughout is light and mocking, as it is also in 'God's Judgement on a Wicked Bishop,' which tells the gruesome story of the hard-hearted Bishop Hatto, who in the midst of famine, refuses to feed the poor from his well-filled granary, but instead invites them to his huge barn and then sets fire to the barn killing all within. For his wickedness he is punished by an army of rats, who swim the river Rhine, consume his corn, and finally attack and consume the Bishop himself. The account in Coryat's *Crudities*, appended to the poem, contains no hint of humor. 'Cornelius Agrippa' is still another ballad in which appropriate punishment is meted out. A young man, employed by the magician Agrippa, reads in a horrible book of magic written upon parchment of human skin, but he is interrupted in his reading by no less a personage than the devil himself, who addresses the young man three times:

'What wouldst thou with me?' the third time he cries,
And a flash of lightning came from his eyes,
And he lifted his griffin claw in the air,
And the young man had not strength for a prayer.

His eyes red fire and fury dart
As out he tore the young man's heart;
He grinn'd a horrible grin at his prey,
And in a clap of thunder vanish'd away.

THE MORAL
Henceforth let all young men take heed
How in a Conjuror's books they read.

Southey's treatment of the devil – or Beelzebub or Satan – deserves a paragraph. He is always the devil of folklore – of Burns's poetry – rather than the fallen angel of Milton's *Paradise Lost*. He is never treated seriously, but humorously, and he himself often speaks with ironical amusement. The devil makes his appearance in 'The Old Woman of Berkeley' and 'Cornelius Agrippa,' and in 'The Pious Painter' the devil is portrayed as vain enough to wish a flattering portrait of himself rather than the traditional sketches given him. In 'St. Antidius, the Pope, and the Devil' the Pope escapes – the reader is not told the reason – from the devil, but the picture of Beelzebub is a lively one:

Oh, then King Beelzebub for joy,
    He drew his mouth so wide,
You might have seen his iron teeth,
    Four and forty from side to side.

> He wagg'd his ears, he twisted his tail,
>   He knew not for joy what to do,
> In his hoofs and his horns, in his heels and his corns,
>   It tickled him all through.

But the longest poem in which the Devil figures is the joint poem with Coleridge called 'The Devil's Walk,' a work revised several times from its initial publication in the *Morning Post* on September 6, 1799, until its final publication in Southey's collected edition in 1838. The devil in this poem is still the same light-hearted, often quizzical person we have seen in Southey's other poems as he walks the streets and observes many a kindred spirit in those he meets: a lady, a lord, a lawyer, an apothecary, a prison turnkey, among others.

Other ballads and metrical tales follow other groupings. A large number are derived from contemporary observations or by stories that came to him in one way or another. Many of these bear a marked resemblance to the poetic fashions of the 1790s and to the tales narrated by Wordsworth in *Lyrical Ballads*. They are tales of distress, of unwarranted suffering, brought about by the inexorableness of economic conditions, or by the effects of the war. Some, however, have no connection with any particular set of contemporary conditions: they are simply part of the human condition and reflect constant and abiding patterns of human behavior. 'The Cross Roads' narrates – an old man tells a soldier – the simple story of a young girl who committed suicide and was buried where four roads meet. 'Mary the Maid of the Inn' and 'Jaspar' describe maniacs. Mary has become so because of her knowledge of the murder her lover Richard had committed and of the hanging he suffered in consequence. Jaspar, however, is one who had been led into crime by poverty, but remorse has maddened him. Parallels with the work of other poets are usually self-evident. Walter Scott was doing many of the same things. Southey's 'Lord William' tells in ballad form of the vengeance of a drowned child upon his murderer – this story of the wicked uncle who had killed the child for his inheritance is much in the vein of Scott's ballads where the dead return to avenge the crimes of which they were the victims. Coleridge's 'Ancient Mariner,' especially in its 'Gothic' and unrevised version of 1798, is likewise in the same vein. The mention of Scott's name is a reminder that Scott admired Southey's tales and was familiar with his verse. Scott was fond of reciting poems, and his phenomenal memory enabled him to memorize a poem after one hearing. Two of his favorites for recitation were 'Queen Orraca and the Five Martyrs of Morocco' and 'The Inchcape Rock.' There is a suspicion that the inaccurate versions of these poems in the poetical department of the *Edinburgh Annual Register* may owe their irregularities – as well as their publication in that place – to the imperfections of Scott's memory since these poems had not at that date been reprinted from the *Post*.

Not all Southey's humorous poems are of the grotesque-horrible category. 'The Well of St. Keyne' is a cheerful version of the old stories concerning the desire of the wife to achieve mastery over her husband – in this instance by drinking from the waters of the well before the ceremony. This wife is successful, but the wife in 'St. Michael's Chair' – the legend there is that the first to sit in the chair will be master – is killed by the unexpected ringing of the bells in the tower where the chair is located. Although Southey virtually stopped writing in this genre by 1805, he occasionally returned to the form, and 'Roprecht the Robber' (1829) with its humorous treatment of the hanging and re-hanging of a notorious robber shows that he had not forgotten the technique and the formula.

From the writing of ballads upon legendary and semi-historical topics it is only a short step to writing tales of contemporary life. Southey's *Poems* of 1797 reveals a whole gallery of life's unfortunates: African slaves, the inhabitants of Botany Bay (the destination of many transported felons), a soldier's wife, a widow, a maniac, a pauper – indeed the outcasts of society. The characters are, of course, kin to those that were to appear in *Lyrical Ballads* in the following year, where the table of contents to that famous work lists such poems as 'The Female Vagrant,' 'The Mad Mother,' 'The Idiot Boy,' and 'The Convict.' It is not so much a matter of one author influencing another – although Southey and Wordsworth were aware of each other's work – but of both poets writing in a popular style and using popular themes that were currently being used by many a poet whose works appeared in the poetical departments of the magazines. To treat such persons seriously and to sympathize with their wrongs were not points of view congenial to those who held to established views of the proper subject matter of literature. The result was that an author became the object of parody and harsh, even vituperative, criticism. A quotation from Francis Jeffrey's review of *Thalaba* in the *Edinburgh Review* (1802), where several pages are devoted to deploring the present tendency of a new sect of poetry to write and to sympathize with these outcasts of society, is both informative and explanatory of this orthodox point of view:

> A splenetic and idle discontent with the existing institutions of
> society, seems to be at the bottom of all their serious and peculiar
> sentiments. . . . For all sorts of vice and profligacy in the lower
> orders of society, they have the same virtuous horror, and the
> same tender compassion. . . . The present vicious constitution of
> society alone is responsible for all these enormities: the poor
> sinners are but the helpless victims or instruments of its disorders,
> and could not possibly have avoided the errors into which they
> have been betrayed. Though they can bear with crimes,
> therefore, they cannot reconcile themselves to punishments; and
> have an unconquerable antipathy to prisons, gibbets, and houses
> of correction, as engines of oppression, and instruments of
> atrocious injustice. . . . If it be natural for a poor man to murder
> and rob, in order to make himself comfortable, it is no less
> natural for a rich man to gormandize and domineer, in order
> to have the full use of his riches. Wealth is just as valid an
> excuse for the one class of vices, as indigence is for the other.
> There are many other peculiarities of false sentiment in the
> productions of this class of writers, that are sufficiently deserving
> of commemoration.

Many of the unfortunates of whom Southey writes would have suffered under any political system; the young girl of 'The Ruined Cottage,' who is 'by a villain's wiles seduced,' or the Mary of 'Mary, the Maid of the Inn,' who is so ill-fated as to love a murderer, but the overwhelming evidence is weighted towards those who suffer, not so much because of bad luck but because of the built-in injustices of the political and legal system. The 'Botany Bay Eclogues' depict a group of characters who have suffered from hardship and were led into a crime through the pressures of want and poverty. Elinor has been 'the hireling prey of brutal appetite' and after want and famine dared 'dishonesty' and was transported. Another convict was transported for poaching, and a sailor and a soldier, after incredible hardships in the service and distress at home after their discharge, resorted to thievery and robbery. But as Frederic said in justification:

> What if I warr'd upon the world? the world
> Had wrong'd me first: I had endur'd the ills

Of hard injustice; all this goodly earth
Was but to me one wild waste wilderness;
I had no share in Nature's patrimony.

Three poems from Southey's 1797 volume were chosen for parody
by George Canning and John Hookham Frere, the clever satirical poets
of the *Anti-Jacobin* (1797–8): 'Inscription for the Apartment in Chepstow Castle,' 'The Widow,' and 'The Soldier's Wife.' 'The Soldier's
Wife' was not only jacobinical in subject but was written in dactylics,
an early attempt of Southey to adapt classical metres to English verse.
The fact that this early exercise in the dactyl proved a convenient
target for the parodist did not deter Southey from the same experiment
a score of years later when he composed his *Vision of Judgment* in
dactylic hexameters which led in turn to Byron's brilliant parody. The
dactyl was a dangerous and unfortunate metre for Southey.

'The Soldier's Wife' and the *Anti-Jacobin* parody are given herewith.
The Soldier's Wife

Weary way-wanderer languid and sick at heart
Travelling painfully over the rugged road,
Wild-visag'd Wanderer! ah for thy heavy chance!

Surely thy little one drags by thee bare-footed,
Cold is the baby that hangs at thy bending back
Meagre and livid and screaming its wretchedness.

Woe-begone mother, half anger, half agony,
As over thy shoulder thou lookest to hush the babe,
Bleakly the blinding snow beats in thy hagged face.★

Thy husband will never return from the war again,
Cold is thy hopeless heart even as Charity –
Cold are thy famish'd babes – God help thee, widow'd one!

And now for the *Anti-Jacobin* parody:

The Soldier's Friend

Come, little Drummer Boy, lay down your knapsack here;
I am the Soldier's Friend – here are some books for you;
Nice clever books by Tom Paine, the philanthropist.

★ This stanza was supplied by S. T. Coleridge.

Here's half-a-crown for you – here are some handbills too –
Go to the Barracks, and give all the Soldiers some:
Tell them the Sailors are all in a Mutiny.
>>> *Exit Drummer Boy, with Handbills and Half-a-crown.*
>>> *Manet Soldier's Friend.*

Liberty's friends thus all learn to amalgamate,
Freedom's volcanic explosion prepares itself,
Despots shall bow to the Fasces of Liberty,
>> Reason, philosophy, 'fiddledum diddledum,'
>> Peace and Fraternity, 'higgledy, piggledy,'
>> Higgledy, piggledy, 'fiddledum, diddledum.'
>>> *Et caetera, et caetera, et caetera.*

A more cheerful group of poems than these dismal personal tragedies
are those in which Southey speaks of himself and his own personal life.
Very few stand out as vigorous works, but they tell us much about
Southey. The 1797 volume also contains such pleasant poems as a
tribute to Mary Wollstonecraft, a poem on his own miniature taken
at the age of two, a poem on a picture by Gaspar Poussin, and the
'Hymn to the Penates,' recording Southey's love of home, fireside,
and domestic pleasures. For a person who was so reserved about many
personal matters and who so preferred private to public life Southey
reveals a good deal of his inner life. 'Written on Christmas Day, 1795'
records his feelings on being a traveller in Spain and away from his
young wife whom he had married the previous month. In the conclusion he addresses her thus:

>> Yes, think of me,
> My Edith, think that, travelling far away,
> Thus I beguile the solitary hours
> With many a day-dream, picturing scenes as fair
> Of peace, and comfort, and domestic bliss
> As ever to the youthful poet's eye
> Creative Fancy fashion'd. Think of me,
> Though absent, thine; and if a sigh will rise,
> And tears, unbidden, at the thought steal down,
> Sure hope will cheer thee, and the happy hour
> Of meeting soon all sorrow overpay.

Several poems record his travels and are little more than versified
travel diaries such as 'Written on Christmas Day,' just cited, and

'Recollections of a Day's Journey in Spain,' as well as the lengthy first part of *The Poet's Pilgrimage to Waterloo* (1816). 'To Charles Lamb' (1830) is a tribute to an old friendship and records with pleasure that Lamb is now receiving the recognition he deserves:

> To us, who have admired and loved thee long,
> It is a proud as well as pleasant thing
> To hear thy good report, now borne along
> Upon the honest breath of public praise;
> We know that with the elder sons of song,
> In honouring whom thou hast delighted still,
> Thy name shall keep its course to after days.

The two most popular of Southey's personal poems are certainly 'The Holly Tree' and 'My days among the dead are past' sometimes called 'Books.' The first is an early work and was first published in the *Morning Post* for December 17, 1798, while the second belongs to 1818. The fourth and seventh stanzas from 'The Holly Tree' will illustrate the way in which he draws a parallel from the tree to himself.

> Thus, though abroad perchance I might appear
>   Harsh and austere,
> To those who on my leisure would intrude
>   Reserved and rude,
> Gentle at home amid my friends I'd be
> Like the high leaves upon the Holly Tree. . . .
>
> So serious should my youth appear among
>   The thoughtless throng,
> So would I seem amid the young and gay
>   More grave than they,
> That in my age as cheerful I might be
> As the green winter of the Holly Tree.

As Southey grew older his days were increasingly spent at the desk in writing and with the books in his library. This library, we have seen, was an amazing one for so poor a man, and visitors remarked its extent and its disposition within a room overlooking mountain and lake. His short poem, sometimes entitled 'Books,' sums up this aspect of Southey's life.

My days among the Dead are past;
  Around me I behold,
Where'er these casual eyes are cast,
  The mighty minds of old;
My never failing friends are they,
With whom I converse day by day.

With them I take delight in weal,
  And seek relief in woe;
And while I understand and feel
  How much to them I owe,
My cheeks have often been bedew'd
With tears of thoughtful gratitude.

My thoughts are with the Dead, with them
  I live in long-past years,
Their virtues love, their faults condemn,
  Partake their hopes and fears,
And from their lessons seek and find
Instruction with an humble mind.

My hopes are with the Dead, anon
  My place with them will be,
And I with them shall travel on
  Through all Futurity;
Yet leaving here a name, I trust,
That will not perish in the dust.

Southey's ability to get on well with children and to enter into their world is an attractive side of his personal life and is recorded, most notably, in his prose classic of 'The Three Bears,' but 'The Cataract of Lodore,' a poem often included in anthologies of poems for children, also reflects this side of his life. The poem is for the most part a clever exercise in rhyming:

Dividing and gliding and sliding,
And falling and brawling and sprawling
And driving and riving and striving,
And sprinkling and twinkling and wrinkling . . .
All at once and all o'er, with a mighty uproar
And this way the Water comes down at Lodore.

Southey found in history stories of action which came ready-made for his poetic purpose. Although he might speak of history (in his short poem 'History') as 'Thou chronicle of crimes' and as filled with a 'court's polluted scenes' and 'dungeon horrors,' he could also find in history scenes of 'nobler feelings' and examples to show a 'deeper love of Freedom.' Indeed, the protagonists of his poems are usually those who have fought for freedom against tyrants and who not infrequently suffered death as the consequence. These subjects he found everywhere: in the Bible, in Greek and Roman history, and especially in the history of Britain from the age of legendary heroes to the eighteenth-century battle of Blenheim. The lesson of these poems is very simple: tyranny and the tyrant must be overcome; the tyrant meets his just doom often by a violent end in which he is tormented by the pangs of conscience (as the French King Henry responsible for the St Bartholomew's Day massacre and the English Henry V in 'King Henry and the Hermit of Dreux'). The hero or heroine dies with the assurance that the cause will triumph and that the sacrifice has been worthwhile. Examples abound. The unnamed monarch in 'The Destruction of Jerusalem,' helpless before the power of Babylon, finds 'the remembered guilt more dreadful than the impending destruction.' Wallace in 'The Death of Wallace' dies on the scaffold confident 'of that good cause for which he died/And that was joy in death.' Lucretia in the mono-drama of that name assures herself of the value of her sacrifice because by that means Brutus will overthrow Tarquin and the tyranny under which Rome has been cringing. Behind all these events there is implied a belief that a Providence rules the events of man and that the just and righteous man will be rewarded, if not in this world, then in the next.

Not all poems classified as historical belong to early times. An unreprinted poem, 'War Poem,' first published in the *Morning Post* for June 22, 1798 and cancelled in most copies of the *Annual Anthology* – celebrated the withdrawal of the English from Toulon and praised the energy of the French:

> For France in all the greatness of her strength
> Comes drunk in wrath, and mighty to destroy!
> Her own right arm hath brought salvation to her.
> Her fury hath upheld her!

'The Victory' describes an individual tale of heroism from the current war. Generally, however, Southey's historical poems are from tradi-tional sources, and sometimes the line between history and legend is a thin one. But the stories that he selects have a lesson for the present and reveal his own point of view.

Certainly the most famous of Southey's poems with an historical bent is 'The Battle of Blenheim' in its strongly pacific and anti-war sentiment. It advances the thesis that war is futile as a means of settling disputes and points out the transitoriness of military glory. The penetrating questions and comments which young Peterkin and Wilhelmine ask their grandfather not only give the reader the interpretation which the author desires but they also reveal an idea associated with Wordsworth that children have insights which their elders have not. Peterkin and Wilhelmine are thus kin to the whole gallery of Wordsworth's perceptive children.

> 'Now tell us what 'twas all about,'
>   Young Peterkin, he cries;
> And little Wilhelmine looks up
>   With wonder-waiting eyes;
> 'Now tell us all about the war,
> And what they fought each other for.'

But grandfather Kaspar can only repeatedly assure them that 'It was a famous victory.'

The inscription – certainly not the most popular poetic form – was one that Southey employed throughout his career. In blank verse, his inscriptions vary in length from twenty to a hundred lines. It was a form ideally suited for newspaper and magazine publication, and it enabled the author to combine a description of a picturesque scene associated with a famous event or historical personage. The inscription thus is closely linked to Southey's poems on historical subjects, but sometimes as in 'Inscription for a Tablet on the Banks of a Stream' it only describes a pleasant spot with no special association. The inscription is similar to the epitaph when it commemorates an individual, and in subject and method of handling is rather like a sonnet, but looser in that the poet is not restricted to a prescribed length or the necessity of rhyme. Southey's volume of *Poems* in 1797 contained a series of eight inscriptions on such diverse historical characters as King John, William the Conqueror, the patriot Algernon Sidney, the poet Sir Philip Sidney, the martyrs Ridley and Latimer, the regicide Henry Marten, the Spanish conquistador Pizarro, and the infamous 'hanging' Judge Jeffries. The selection of persons is significant since most were either defiers or perpetrators of tyranny. Years later Southey wrote a series of inscriptions to record the places in Spain associated with the heroic deeds of the Spaniards and their British allies during the Peninsular War. Finally, in 1829 Southey wrote the 'Inscriptions for the Caledonian Canal' in commemoration of his tour through Scotland in the company of his old friend John Rickman and Thomas Telford, the engineer to whose genius the canal was owing.

An interesting aspect of Southey's poetry during the first decade of his writing is a group of poems concerning women. Southey admired the woman of spirit, intelligence, and determination, especially when exerted in a good cause, and in another age would have been an active participant in the movement for women's rights. As it was, he was a great admirer of Mary Wollstonecraft, whose book, *A Vindication of the Rights of Woman*, he had read soon after its publication in 1792. He opened his *Poems* (1797) with a short, complimentary poem to her and followed it by a narrative from the apocryphal book of Esdras entitled 'The Triumph of Woman,' in which a song in praise of the power of woman results in the order of Darius for the rebuilding of the temple in Jerusalem. Southey's poems abound in brave, intelligent, and determined women. The selection of Joan of Arc as the subject for his first poem was not accidental, and her triumph in providing the leadership for her country in defeating the foreign foe was a lesson for the day. The French Revolution was not without its heroines, and Southey admired such courageous spirits as Charlotte Corday, the murderess of Marat. A quick glance at the list of poems reveals a host of heroines: Sappho, Lucretia, the wife of Fergus who exults over her own slaying of her husband, and Joan. There is not a weakling in the lot and, save for Sappho, all have a commitment to liberty and oppose tyrannical rule.

During the twenty years during which Southey wrote most of his poetry there is no doubt that he was a revolutionary poet, if by that phrase we mean that he was a poet who had turned away from the traditional neo-classic concerns and was willing to experiment in all metres and to follow the new fashion of writing about persons in humble and rustic life as well as those outcasts of society whom polite persons ignored. It was very much part of the *avant-garde* movement of the day, and so many writers were following these new trends that a conservative critic such as Francis Jeffrey was – according to his standards – rightly alarmed at the rise of this new sect of poetry that was challenging the poetical orthodoxy. But if there were detractors there were also supporters. John Aikin of the *Monthly Magazine* welcomed new things, and Coleridge, Lamb, and William Taylor approved of what Southey was doing. Not everything that Southey tried was successful, but the trend of the times was with him. New forms of writing, new subjects, and a new generation of writers treated seriously and with respect persons from every walk of life. The child, the maniac, the prisoner, the transported felon, the poor, and the outcast were equally held in honor.

But the literature of the day was also fascinated by the exotic and the remote. On a small scale Southey had explored the past in his ballads and had delighted in macabre stories. On a larger scale he ranged far afield in the next four poems to be discussed. In *Thalaba* Southey takes his readers to a strange world of Arabian fiction; in *Madoc* to medieval Wales and the establishment of a colony in the midst of the heathenish American Aztecs; in *The Curse of Kehama* to the mysterious world of Hindu mythology; and it is only in *Roderick* that he comes to the familiar world of European Christendom, but that world too is remote in time, set as it is in the midst of conflict between Christian and Moor in medieval Spain.

9

Long Poems: *Thalaba, Madoc, Kehama, Roderick*

The long poems of Southey, often called epics, might better be described as narrative poems. *Thalaba the Destroyer*, published in 1801, was derived from Arabian sources. The plot is uncomplicated, but the poem is peopled with numerous demonic and angelic figures as well as the use of magic rings, oaths, and curses. Thalaba, the hero and sole survivor of his family, is assigned the duty of avenging the death of his father Hodeirah, whom Okba, one of the demons dwelling in the cave of Dom Daniel, had killed. The demons know that Thalaba is the man of destiny who is to destroy them, and they seek his destruction before he can effect his mission. The family of Moath befriend Thalaba, and he grows from boyhood to manhood with them, falling in love with Moath's daughter Oneiza. Thalaba, when he is grown, departs on his mission which leads him through the ruins of Babylon and many a desert, valley, and mountain. He is protected by a magic ring which he had obtained after his encounter with the demon Abdaldar. However, he later throws away the ring to the commendation of the angels Maruth and Haruth who assure him 'Son of Hodeirah! thou hast proved it here; the Talisman is Faith.' Thalaba withstands temptations of wine and women in a cave rather reminiscent of Spenser's Bower of Bliss, and is finally united in marriage with Oneiza, but the Angel of Death takes her from him on the wedding night. On one of his further journeys Thalaba meets Laila, the daughter of Okba, who, in a struggle between her father and Thalaba, receives the fatal blow her father intended for Thalaba. Thalaba finally reaches the cave of Dom Daniel, is successful in his struggle, but when the opportunity comes to kill Okba – the vengeance to which he had been appointed – he pardons him instead. Thalaba's final action is to plunge his sword into the idol Eblis which, as it falls, destroys everything. The poem ends with the death of Thalaba as Oneiza's form welcomes him to 'eternal bliss.'

The story of Thalaba is the familiar one of the quest in which the hero successfully performs an incredible number of difficult tasks, being both aided and deterred by supernatural persons and forces. The reader's interest, however, is not so much in Thalaba's actual adventures as in the development of his character as he learns the lesson that he must give up the use of magic, represented by the ring of Abdaldar, substitute faith for magic, and pardon rather than avenge. The lesson of the poem is made clear at the end when the voice of the Prophet declares:

> Thou hast done well my Servant!
> Ask and receive thy reward!

The reception of the poem was mixed. Jeffrey's review in the *Edinburgh Review* was only partly concerned with *Thalaba*. Jeffrey objected to the remoteness of the poem from the real concerns of men and society, to its experimental metre, and to the unfamiliarity of the Arabian legends on which the poem was founded. Readers, however, of a younger generation than Southey's responded to the appeal of the poem. The figure of Thalaba, a young man whose life was solely dedicated to a quest and a holy mission, strongly appealed to the idealistic young Shelley and to the young John Henry Newman. In 1850 Newman recalled that 'Thalaba has ever been to my feelings the most sublime of English poems – I mean *morally* sublime. And his [Southey's] poems generally end, not with a marriage, but with death and future glory.' And according to the testimony of his *Apologia* the poem had a share in helping him to a decision during the years of personal crisis in 1832–3 – 'now too, that Southey's beautiful poem of Thalaba, for which I had an immense liking, came forcibly to my mind. I began to think that I had a mission.'

Madoc, the longest and least interesting of Southey's long poems, was begun as early as 1794, discarded, and not resumed until many years later. The poem is in two parts and tells a complicated story. Madoc, a twelfth-century prince, has founded a colony in the new world, and has defeated the Aztec Indians. He returns to Wales in quest of new followers and tells the story of his adventures. The Welshmen under Madoc had defeated the Aztecs, but instead of seeking revenge by slaughtering their enemies, had made a compact with them that the Aztecs would abandon their practice of demanding human sacrifice. The second part, Madoc in Aztlan, describes the attempts of the priests to reassert the old ways, and the efforts of Madoc, the Welshmen, and their Indian allies to thwart the revolt. Many of the incidents are truly horrible with accounts of thousands of human sacrifices. Madoc is finally successful in defeating the Aztecs, but the climax of the struggle coincides with the eruption of a volcano. The poem is in some sense a missionary poem in which Madoc, the Christian missionary, attempts to convert the heathen Aztecs from their idolatrous ways. The poem, like *Thalaba*, is heavily indebted to many travel books and accounts of the religious rites of the Americans, and the notes are voluminous.

The faults of *Madoc* are transparent. The two parts of the poem lack unity, and the length – nine thousand lines – is unjustified. The first part is concerned with Welsh affairs, and Madoc, as a Welsh prince, might well have found work enough to do by straightening out affairs in that troubled kingdom. But instead of so doing, he sets out for the new world and involves himself in the affairs of the Aztecs. The characters are many and are usually sketched in terms of good and bad; they are 'flat' rather than 'round.' But there are still some good things. The description at the opening of the second part of the village of Caermadoc is attractive as a kind of idealized settlement in the new world – the dream of pantisocracy realized for a brief moment. The scenes in the Welsh court have a certain charm, and Southey utilizes to good advantage that constant element in all tales of medieval times – the minstrel. This use of the minstrel suggests Scott's use of an old minstrel in *The Lay of the Last Minstrel* published like *Madoc* in 1805. Southey's failure, artistic and commercial, can be contrasted with Scott's popular success. Scott's story of medieval days in Scotland had the slightest of plots, but was varied by the use of popular superstitions familiar to most readers and by the introduction of short lyrics. Southey's story of medieval times was of great complexity and involved material that almost no reader could be expected to know. Scott's technique of having a minstrel of comparatively recent days tell the story of an earlier time gives unity to the poem, and the introduction of the old minstrel from time to time breaks the tedium of the narrative. Scott's characters are few in number and have familiar names, not such strange names as those of Coatel, Yuhidthiton, or Amahlata. Both poems contained many antiquarian footnotes, but although a reader can ignore Scott's, a certain number of Southey's are really necessary to understanding the poem.

Although the reception and sale of *Madoc* were disappointing, there were readers and reviewers who praised. Scott read the poem three times, each time with increasing admiration, and William Taylor pronounced it the best poem since *Paradise Lost*. Both Dorothy and William Wordsworth read the poem with pleasure, but remarked that the character of Madoc was not sufficiently heroic for the hero of such a poem. They preferred the character Llewellyn, and Wordsworth admired a passage describing the meeting of the bards:

> His eyes were closed;
> His head, as if in reverence to receive
> The inspiration, bent; and as he raised
> His glowing Countenance and brighter eye
> And swept with passionate hands the ringing harp.

The discouraging sale of *Madoc* led Southey to set aside his writing of *The Curse of Kehama*, but his meeting with Landor in 1808 led him to resume its composition, and when published in 1810, the poem was appropriately dedicated to Landor. *The Curse of Kehama* is thought by some critics – notably Southey's biographer Simmons – to be Southey's best. The poem suffers from the same fault as *Thalaba* and *Madoc* in that the background is not familiar to most readers, but Southey is more skilful in overcoming that handicap. The characters and incidents are fewer in number, and, although the stanzas are of irregular length, like *Thalaba*, they are rhymed, and the introduction of several short lyrics gives variety to the prosodic pattern. The opening of the poem is striking and describes the gorgeous pageantry of the funeral of Arvalan with its long procession of priests, mourners, and finally the wives and slaves who are to be burnt with Arvalan on the funeral pyre. The climax of the event is well told:

> Then hand in hand the victim band
> Roll in the dance around the funeral pyre;
> Their garments' flying folds
> Float inward to the fire;
> In drunken whirl they wheel around;
> One drops . . . another plunges in;
> And still with overwhelming din
> The tambours and the trumpets sound;
> And clap of hand, and shouts, and cries,
> From all the multitude arise;

While round and round, in giddy wheel,
    Intoxicate they roll and reel,
Till one by one whirl'd in they fall,
And the devouring flames have swallow'd all.

The story of *Kehama* concerns three mortals and a group of immortals.
Arvalan, son of the rajah Kehama, has been killed by Ladurlad, who
had attempted to seize his daughter Kailyal. Ladurlad, instead of being
executed, receives a curse from Kehama. Kailyal effects her own escape.
The curse, often reprinted, is an effective bit of incantatory poetry.

    I charm thy life
From the weapons of strife,
From stone and from wood,
   From fire and from flood,
   From the serpent's tooth,
   And the beasts of blood:
From Sickness I charm thee,
And Time shall not harm thee;
   But Earth which is mine,
   Its fruits shall deny thee;
   And Water shall hear me,
And know thee and fly thee;
And the Winds shall not touch thee
   When they pass by thee,
And the Dews shall not wet thee,
When they shall fall nigh thee:
And thou shalt seek Death
   To release thee, in vain;
Thou shalt live in thy pain
While Kehama shall reign,
   With a fire in thy heart,
   And a fire in thy brain;
   And Sleep shall obey me,
   And visit thee never,
And the Curse shall be on thee
   For ever and ever.

The rajah Kehama is an ambitious ruler who seeks dominion not only
on earth but in heaven and hell. Southey pointed out in his preface
that prayers, penances, and sacrifices in the religion of the Hindoos are
a kind of draft upon Heaven, and payment cannot be refused. Thus it is

that the worst of men can obtain power that makes them 'formidable to the Supreme Deities themselves.' This belief became the foundation of the poem. Kehama's boundless ambition, his cruelty, and his determination to succeed make him a counterpart of Napoleon. *The Curse of Kehama* will not bear an allegorical interpretation, but the two careers of Kehama and Napoleon have parallels. During the time Southey was composing his poem and at the time of its publication in 1810 Napoleon was seemingly invincible, and the lesson of the poem is an encouraging one for the times; namely, that tyranny is not permanent and the worst of situations will come to an end.

The poem, after the opening scenes and the pronouncement of the curse, describes the journeys and trials of both Ladurlad and Kailyal, sometimes together, and sometimes when they are separated from each other. Although Arvalan, son of Kehama, had been killed and duly buried, his spirit still seeks to gain possession of Kailyal, but he is always thwarted. Kehama's curse becomes a blessing for Ladurlad because he is immune from death and from the normally fatal effects of fire, water, and the sword, and thus he is able to save Kailyal from various perils. Kehama finally succeeds in gaining control of Heaven or Swerga and then plans the conquest of Padalon or hell. But when Kehama drinks the amreeta, the cup of immortality, he finds that by an ironical reversal he has drunk of death and punishment and becomes one of the four supporters of the throne of Yamen, the king or ruler of hell. When, however, Kailyal drinks the cup, she is transported to the Bower of Bliss to enjoy immortality as Ladurlad sinks to rest and awakes in heaven.

Although the poem is based upon the idea that it is possible for a mortal to conquer worlds outside this world, forces above and beyond these powers have a greater sway. Padalon with its figures of Yamen and Baly is not only a place of punishment, but also of judgment of good as well as evil. The picture of Yamen in the twenty-third book makes this explicit:

> Behold him as the King
> Of Terrors, black of aspect, red of eye, . . .
> But to the righteous Spirit how benign
> His aweful countenance,
> Where, tempering justice with parental love,
> Goodness and heavenly grace
> And sweetest mercy shine!

It is in Padalon that justice finally triumphs with punishment for the presumptuous tyrant Kehama and the rewards of immortality and rest for the virtuous and long-suffering Kailyal and Ladurlad.

Other effective characters are Ereenia, a Glendoveer who lives in the Swerga, and the witch Lorrinite. Ereenia, an Ariel-like and benevolent creature, seems to love Kailyal in his ethereal way, and transports her through the skies in a heavenly car to the Bower of Bliss and the throne of Indra. The description of Ereenia suggests the designs of William Blake, and it is interesting to speculate what Blake could have done in illustrating the poem. Although not human, Ereenia assumes a human form, and is described thus (Book VII):

And never yet did form more beautiful,
   In dreams of night descending from on high,
Bless the religious Virgin's gifted sight,
     Nor like a vision of delight,
Rise on the raptured Poet's inward eye.
     Of human form divine was he,
The immortal Youth of Heaven who floated by,
Even such as that divinest form shall be
In those blest stages of our onward race,
       When no infirmity,
  Low thought, nor base desire, nor wasting care,
Deface the semblance of our heavenly sire.

The passage suggests two stanzas – with the echo of the phrase 'human form divine' of Blake's 'The Divine Image':

For Mercy, Pity, Peace, and Love
  Is God, our father dear;
And Mercy, Pity, Peace, and Love
  Is Man, his child and care.

For Mercy has a human heart,
  Pity a human face,
And love, the human form divine;
  And Peace, the human dress.

Ereenia's actions in the poem exhibit the qualities of mercy, pity, and love. Ereenia seems closer to a Blake creation than to the very human characters of Scott's and Byron's poetry.

The sinister witch Lorrinite is finely described in the eleventh book entitled 'The Enchantress,' and the chanted dialogue between Lorrinite and Arvalan provides welcome metrical variation:

> Comest thou, son, for aid to me?
>> Tell me who have injured thee,
>> Where they are, and who they be:
>>> Of the Earth, or of the Sea,
>>>> Or of the aerial company?
> Earth, nor Sea, nor Air is free
> From the powers who wait on me,
>> And my tremendous witchery.

The lesson of *The Curse of Kehama* is that faith, fortitude, and righteousness will triumph, and the poem makes clear that powers in the universe will ultimately see that justice is done. The characters Kailyal, Ladurlad, and Ereenia are firm in this belief, and the poet so reminds the reader at appropriate intervals. In the tenth book the poet speaks of the permanence of love:

> They sin who tell us Love can die,
>> With life all other passions fly,
>>> All others are but vanity.
> In Heaven Ambition cannot dwell,
>> Nor Avarice in the vaults of Hell;
>> Earthly these passions of the Earth,
> They perish where they have their birth;
>>>> But Love is indestructible.
>> Its holy flame for ever burneth,
> From Heaven it came, to Heaven returneth;
>> Too oft on Earth a troubled guest,
>>> At times deceived, at times opprest,
>>>> It here is tried and purified,
> Then hath in Heaven its perfect rest:
>> It soweth here with toil and care,
> But the harvest time of Love is there.

In this book Ereenia instructs Ladurlad and Kailyal about tyranny and oppression in other times and how it had been overthrown. They learn the lesson well:

> Thus was Ladurlad's soul imbued
>> With hope and holy fortitude;

And Child and Sire, with pious mind,
   Alike resolved, alike resign'd,
  Look'd onward to the evil day:
 Faith was their comfort, Faith their stay;
 They trusted woe would pass away,
  And Tyranny would sink subdued,
   And Evil yield to Good.

The lessons for persons living in the year 1810 when the tyranny and success of Napoleon knew no bounds were likewise apparent. *The Curse of Kehama* can be read as a poem with a message of hope and a faith that there is a Providence guiding the affairs of men. Of poets contemporary with Southey, Shelley echoed some of the same views. His *Revolt of Islam* (1818) and *Prometheus Unbound* (1820) contain many elements in common with this poem: the description of heaven, the air, and earth and the message of hope. Indeed Shelley scholars have pointed out these parallels.

A reader who has not read any of Southey's long poems might start with *The Curse of Kehama,* and if its oriental setting and images of earth, air, heaven, and hell please him, turn next to *Thalaba,* a poem with somewhat similar setting and imagery. If, however, he prefers a poem with a more familiar setting and with human characters, he should turn to *Roderick, the Last of the Goths* (1814).

Roderick, published in 1814, was in Southey's own opinion, his best. The successful struggle in Spain against the power of Napoleon had excited the hearts and imaginations of most Englishmen and led to an interest in all things Spanish. Southey, by virtue of his knowledge of the literature and history of the Peninsula, had already been able to put this knowledge to good use. Other writers also turned to Spanish topics, and Landor and Scott had likewise treated the legend of Roderick, Landor in his *Count Julian* (1812) and Scott in his *Vision of Don Roderick* (1811).

The plot of Southey's poem concerns the series of adventures by which Roderick, the former king, helped to subdue the Moors and restore the kingdom to Spanish rule under Pelayo. Roderick, when king, had dishonored Florinda, daughter of Count Julian, and in revenge Julian called the Moors into Spain, Roderick in consequence losing his throne. The poem opens with Roderick in hiding and in penitence. He assumes the name of Father Maccabee and the garb of a monk and vows to seek the liberation of his country:

Herein I place
My penance for the past, my hope to come,
My faith and my good works; here offer up
All thoughts and passions of mine inmost heart,
My days and night, . . this flesh, this blood, this life,
Yea this whole being, do I here devote
For Spain.

(IV, 18–24)

Under his disguise Roderick goes to the Moorish camp and persuades Pelayo to escape and lead the Christian forces. Roderick and Pelayo are successful at the battle of Covadonga, Roderick disappears, and Pelayo rules as king of Spain.

This brief outline reveals a unified action that moves in a straight line to its conclusion. In an historical sense Pelayo is the central figure since he becomes king and wins the battle of Covadonga, but the poem, however, centers not upon Pelayo but upon Roderick, his struggles with himself, and his contribution to the fight against the Moors and in support of Pelayo. At the opening of the poem Roderick is in despair, but at the end he has triumphed over his despair. This inward triumph of Roderick is parallel to the outward triumph of Pelayo, but there is a paradox in this triumph because he has achieved it only by yielding the power he once had and giving up all thought of regaining his former position. Unlike such heroes of Southey's earlier poems as Thalaba and Ladurlad, Roderick is a very human person in that he has sinned. His violation of Florinda had led to the invasion of the Moors, to the ruin of Spain as well as the loss of his own royal power. Roderick is in deep despair as the poem opens, and the poem records his success in overcoming his feelings of guilt and remorse. His journeys through the country reveal to him the devastation his actions had produced, and these sights only intensify his feelings. He is so disfigured by his sufferings and self-imposed penitence that he is unrecognized and so pitiful in appearance that he receives alms from the passers-by. His first step in his rehabilitation is to become a priest, and he assumes the name of Father Maccabee. Roderick discovers that many Spaniards will support a fight to throw off Moorish rule, and his first success comes when he persuades Pelayo to accept the call and assume the leadership. Pelayo and Florinda, prisoners of the Moors, escape and join the rebel forces. Roderick's meeting with Florinda is very moving as, in his role of priest, he hears her confession in which she maintains that she has always loved Roderick. Ironically, the knowledge comes too late. Another test for Roderick occurs at the scene of Pelayo's coronation as he perceives the contrast between his former and present states. Roderick, with another irony, finds peace with himself as he renounces all hopes of future power. He explained these feelings to his mother Rusilla, who had suggested that he might some day be restored to the throne:

> Dreams such as thine pass now
> Like evening clouds before me; if I think
> How beautiful they seem, 'tis but to feel
> How sooon they fade, how fast the night shuts in.

And Rusilla assures him of the rightness of his decision:

> Thou hast chosen
> The better part. Yes, Roderick, even on earth
> There is a praise above the monarch's fame,
> A higher, holier, more enduring praise,
> And this will yet be thine!

Renunciation, however, is not easy for Roderick. When he recognizes his old horse Orelio bearing the villain Orpas, his old love of battle is aroused. He causes Orelio to throw Orpas, quickly kills him, mounts Orelio, takes the shield and sword of Count Julian, and is everywhere successful, his success culminating in saving the life of Pelayo, who was engaged in a mortal combat with Sisibert. This series of spectacular martial actions results in the recognition of Roderick, and the cry goes up 'Roderick the Goth! Roderick and Victory!' But with victory gained and the Spaniards victorious, Roderick disappears. Years later a tomb was found

> which bore inscribed
> In ancient characters King Roderick's name.

This combination of conflicting desires in Roderick makes it possible for the reader to respond to him as he never could to such a faultless character as Thalaba. A culpable hero, Roderick ultimately achieves his own peace through renunciation of the means by which men usually hope for satisfaction – power, glory, love, wealth, fame.

The other characters in the poem seem rather pale. The villains are simply sketched as evil men. Pelayo is only a paste-board hero, but Count Julian, through his change of heart and last-minute repentance, becomes more interesting. Adosinda, the wife and mother bent on vengeance, is forcefully drawn, and her appearance is picturesquely described. Alphonso, young son of Count Pedro, is a conventionally drawn young warrior. Two of the finest portrayals are not of persons but of Roderick's dog Theron and horse Orelio, who have no difficulty in penetrating his disguise. Indeed, it was Theron's recognition of Roderick that made his own mother, Rusilla, suspect that the mysterious stranger was really her son.

The blank verse of *Roderick* is unrelieved by any lyrical interludes, but the reader's attention is not, as in *Thalaba* and the *Curse of Kehama*, diverted by metrical experimentation. The poem lacks many high points, but there are some good descriptions especially of picturesque mountains, castles, and battles. The coronation of Pelayo (Book 18) is strikingly presented, and Adosinda's vow (Book 12) to expel the Moorish invaders is dramatic. The last three books (23–25) describing the battle of Covadonga are effective descriptions of battle bringing the poem to a strong conclusion with the righting of old wrongs and the liberation of Spain.

Roderick is a poem marked by reconciliation. As Roderick grows from despair to a peaceful renunciation his path is made easier for him by a number of reconciliations. Through his meeting with Florinda he discovers her affection for him. He becomes the supporter of Pelayo, who under other circumstances could have been his adversary; he is reunited with his mother Rusilla, who accepts his decision to seek no restoration of power; at the end Count Julian is reconciled to Roderick, returns to the Christian fold, and dies as a Christian. Last of all, Roderick, through his heroic actions at the battle, enables Spain to be healed of its divisive wounds as various factions unite under the new king Pelayo.

Roderick gives the reader a feeling of affirmation. Wrongs are made right: the daughter is reconciled to her father; the apostate Julian returns to the Christian faith which he had abjured; and finally Roderick himself through his actions and sacrifices atones for all the injuries he had brought, unintentionally or unwittingly, upon his country. Truth and justice do prevail, and the reader in 1814 might feel that the lesson of the poem was still valid: for had not Spain overthrown the tyranny of Napoleon, even as Roderick and Pelayo had overthrown the tyranny of the Moors?

10

Laureate Odes and Other Poems

It is difficult to say very much in favor of the odes that Southey wrote as laureate. It was ironic that he received this official recognition just as he was turning away from poetry and in the very year (1813) of his outstanding prose success in *The Life of Nelson*. That he was the first poet of any stature whatsoever to receive the post within a century gave the office an importance it had not enjoyed, but for Southey himself it is questionable whether the post brought him a corresponding honor. Great poetry is seldom written on command or in connection with an official duty. Southey's official odes partake more of prose or stately declamation than of poetry. The subject matter of an official poem was bound to be distasteful to his contemporaries who were critical of the monarchy since poems upon state occasions of necessity praised the deeds of kings, queens, and generals.

Kenneth Hopkins in his *Poets Laureate* praises Southey's first official ode, *Carmen Triumphale, For the Commencement of the Year 1814*. Hopkins calls it 'a vigorous and on the whole successful piece,' but a poem whose reception depended upon faction rather than merit. The poem gave Southey the opportunity to recapitulate the long, deter-mined opposition of Britain to Napoleon and his pleasure in that outcome. A diligent reader can find in the other odes matters of interest, but little to move and nothing to enchant. In his 'Ode Written During the War with America, 1814' Southey expressed his sorrow at the 'unnatural strife' of the war with the United States and hoped for a speedy end. He has harsh words for those officials of the government who

> with vain ambition drunk,
> And insolent in wrong,
> Afflict with their misrule the indignant land

> Where Washington hath left
> His awful memory
> A light for after-times!

This ode then mentions causes to which the nation might better address itself such as education (under the auspices of the Church) and emigration whereby the English language and spirit would be spread from the shores of Ontario to the islands of the Pacific.

The best known of the laureate odes, *A Vision of Judgment* (1821), brought forth Byron's masterpiece of the same title. Scenes of heaven and of final judgment are difficult if not impossible for a modern poet, and the portrayal of such scenes is to invite scepticism or, at worst, derision and laughter. Byron's response was, of course, satirical and derisive. The quarrel between Byron and Southey was of long standing, and whatever the misunderstandings that contributed to it, both men were sincere in their conviction about their own rectitude. Oddly enough, the charge against Byron in the preface to the *Vision* concerning the lasciviousness of his poetry was the same one that Southey had made fifteen years earlier against Thomas Moore for the tendency of his poems, and Southey's preface lifts sentences and paragraphs from his review of Moore's in the *Annual Review* for 1806 (Emily Lorraine de Montluzin, 'Southey's "Santanic School" Remarks: An Old Charge for a New Offender,' *Keats-Shelley Journal*, XXI-XXII (1972-3), pp. 29–33). It was, however, the poem and not the preface that Byron parodied in his poem although the satire against Southey was as personal as that which Southey directed against Byron in the preface.

It is impossible to say anything on behalf of Southey's *Vision* as to its general conception and execution, but there are none the less a few good passages in the poem. The opening of the poem, which provides a sample of his use of the hexameter in English, is a fine description of the Lake District from his study window:

> 'Twas at that sober hour when the light of day is receding,
> And from surrounding things the hues wherewith day has
>   adorned them
> Fade, like the hopes of youth, till the beauty of earth is departed:
> Pensive, though not in thought, I stood at the window, beholding
> Mountain and lake and vale; the valley disrobed of its verdure;
> Derwent retaining yet from eve a glassy reflection
> Where his expanded breast, then still and smooth as a mirror,
> Under the woods reposed: the hills that, calm and majestic,

Lifted their heads in the silent sky, from far Glaramar,
Bleacrag, and Maidenmawr, to Grizedal and westermost Withop.
Dark and distinct they rose. The clouds had gather'd above them
High in the middle air, huge, purple, pillowy masses,
While in the west beyond was the last pale tint of the twilight.

Any admirer of Southey can only regret that the poem was ever written, and that Southey's sense of humor, evident in many of his poems, seemed to have left him completely whenever he performed his duty as laureate.

A few comments can be made about some of his last poems. His 'Epistle to Allan Cunningham' contains a notable and humorous description of the various portraits he sat for, and his 'Dedication of . . . The Progress and Prospects of Society' gave him the chance for a final sincere tribute to the memory of his uncle Mr Hill. The old fondness for strange stories buried in old histories never quite left him, and three poems from the latter years – 'Queen Mary's Christening,' 'Roprecht the Robber,' and 'The Young Dragon' – showed that his hand had not lost its cunning. 'The Young Dragon' is the finest of the three and humorously recounts a struggle between a Christian and a pagan in the ancient city of Antioch and how a Christian maid was saved from the young dragon, a fire-eating monster and offspring of the old dragon himself.

II

An Estimate of Southey's Poetry

Southey's rank as a poet must be below that of the highest rank and below that of his contemporaries Blake, Wordsworth, Coleridge, Byron, Shelley, and Keats. But his success and achievement in poetry is perhaps greater and more significant than is sometimes accorded him. A poet who has written even a few poems remembered after a century and a half is not quite a forgotten figure. His successes, however, are far fewer than might have been expected and as his contemporaries – and he himself – predicted. The nagging question of the cause of this failure remains. Part of the reason is due to his truly amazing facility in composing verses and his unwillingness to give his poems the kind of ruthless revision and rewriting which they demanded. Part of this seeming carelessness was due to the pressure of writing for money and the difficulties of his personal life around 1800 when his poetic creativity was at its height, but a more significant cause was a reluctance to involve himself emotionally in the hard thought that must go into the writing of poetry. It was, for instance, easier to write a poem out of the materials of humble and rustic life than it was to exhaust himself – as Wordsworth often did – in seeking to penetrate all the implications of the chosen subject. Although Southey's poems are technically of a high order of competence, they do not go very much beyond the level of high competence. They do not glow with that white incandescence which one finds in the best work of his great contemporaries. Part of the difficulty lay within his own make-up. From his childhood his feelings were acute, and he seems to have sought to protect himself from the ill effects of too intense feelings. He recalled in 1797 his own childhood:

> My feelings were very acute; they used to amuse themselves by making me cry at sad songs and dismal stories. . . . I cannot

now hear a melancholy tale in silence, but I have learnt to whistle (*New Letters*, vol. I, pp. 149–50).

William Taylor once observed to Southey (March 4, 1799):
You have a mimosa-sensibility, which agonizes in so slight a blast; an imagination excessively accustomed to summon up trains of melancholy ideas, and marshal funeral processions; a mind too fond by half, for its own comfort, of sighs and sadness, of pathetic emotions and heart-rending woe.

To which Southey replied:

Once, indeed, I had a mimosa-sensibility, but it has long been rooted out: five years ago I counteracted Rousseau by dieting upon Godwin and Epictetus; they did me some good, but time has done more. I have a dislike to all strong emotion, and avoid whatever could excite it; a book like 'Werter' gives me now unmingled pain. In my own writings you may observe that I rather dwell upon what affects than what agitates (*Memoir . . . Taylor*, 1844, vol. I, pp. 256, 262).

However desirable it may be for the mental health of the individual, a poet cannot rigorously exclude what 'agitates' and avoid whatever tends to excite emotion. This decision of Southey to curb his mimosa-sensibility, wise though it undoubtedly was, may be the root cause of his relative failure as a poet and his greater success as a writer of prose. There is, however, a mystery about genius, its presence or its absence, and the explanation is always elusive.

12

Conclusion

An estimate of Southey as man and author is not easy. Two factors in particular work against his reputation in the present century: he was the object of sustained and brilliant attacks by such writers as Hazlitt and Byron, whose fame has survived untarnished and undiminished; and he also wrote far too much in prose as well as in poetry. It is, therefore, all too easy to accept the words of Southey's detractors as the truth because the sheer length and quantity of his writing serve as a deterrent to reading his works.

The present study has said something about almost every book that Southey wrote and has recommended what might be read with pleasure and profit. But to come to terms with this most prolific of English authors, the reader must take the first step. For this first step, the ballads and metrical tales among his short poems can be recommended, and *Roderick* among his long narrative poems. The prose has many good things to offer. First of all, *The Life of Nelson*, in its entirety; the *Letters from England by Don Manuel Alvarez Espriella* can be enjoyed if the reader is willing to skip topics that fail to interest him; much of the *Colloquies* remains interesting if, again, the reader will skip; and, finally, a selection from the letters – these cannot fail to interest. Southey's prose is probably the easiest to read of any written during his generation. He sought his models in such early eighteenth-century writers as Swift and Defoe, and turned his back on Samuel Johnson and the late eighteenth-century writers. Nor did he search – like Lamb – for models in the seventeenth century. His is a workaday prose adapted for the man whose profession was literature and whose main source of income came from writing for reviews and magazines.

While it would be unrealistic to expect that Southey will ever be rehabilitated into a major figure of English literature, he is none the less a figure of importance in that history: he did much by his personal example as well as his writings both in poetry and prose to advance the movement in England loosely called the Romantic Movement and to enhance the reputation of the literary man in society. He was very much in tune with the new currents of the age. Although he is a writer of talent rather than genius, his writing is always workmanlike and competent. He is, in short, a professional man of letters. All the actions of his life show that he did not turn from the life of authorship to which he was dedicated. As various honors came to him during his maturity and later years, he refused them all, accepting only the honorary D.C.L. from Oxford, but declining offers of a professorship at Durham, of a librarianship at the Advocates' Library in Edinburgh, of a seat in Parliament, and finally – most grand of all – a baronetcy.

Southey's work is at its best when it touches upon the lives of English readers and when he writes of subjects about which an English-speaking reader has knowledge. Far too often, however, he wrote of themes derived from Hindu mythology, American Indian history, and Spanish-Portuguese history, subjects all pretty remote from the interests of the English reader. Sir Walter Scott – the nearest writer to Southey in many of his interests – never made that mistake for his works, however antiquarian or laden with learned annotation, were always in the tradition of British-American civilization.

It is worth noting that writers whose interests are in history and social life and customs rather than literature, find Southey's character, personality, and writings of considerable value and interest. A possible explanation of this phenomenon is that they are unaware of literary and biographical anecdote and of the judgments of the Hazlitt-Byron-Hunt circles and so approach Southey for the light which his writings can throw upon the age and its problems. In general, they like what they find, seeing in his works much of value and relevance.

Southey's life was in many ways a hard one, for it was only by systematic and unremitting work at his desk that he was able to do so much and to provide himself and his family with a living. He was never fortunate in producing a work that commanded a great sale as did the novels and poems of Scott. The career, whatever hardships it entailed, had, however, its compensations. He achieved a position which enabled him to know some of the best and wisest men of his day – not only such literary men as Coleridge, Wordsworth, Scott, and Landor – but such men as Sir George Beaumont, the patron of the arts, Dr Thomas Arnold, who lived nearby at Fox How, Henry Crabb Robinson, the lawyer and diarist, Dr Andrew Bell, the inventor of the

Madras system of education, Thomas Clarkson, the friend of the slaves, John Rickman, the statistician, Sir Humphry Davy, the chemist. Others sought him out such as the young Thomas Carlyle and John Stuart Mill, the American Hispanic scholar, George Ticknor, and in later years the Prime Ministers George Canning and Sir Robert Peel. Men and women prominent in the next generation were attracted to Southey through his writings – such figures as J. H. Newman, W. E. Gladstone, Lord John Manners, and Charlotte Brontë, who exchanged letters with him. It is, all in all, an admirable achievement worthy of honor and of study.

Bibliography

Bibliography

The New Cambridge Bibliography of English Literature (1969) contains the fullest
listing of Southey's works as well as books and articles about him.
For a discussion of the scholarship about Southey see Kenneth Curry, 'Southey,'
English Romantic Poets and Essayists: A Review of Research, ed C. W. and
L. H. Houtchens, revised ed., New York, 1966.

Southey's Principal Works

(place of publication is London unless otherwise stated)
The Fall of Robespierre: An Historic Drama, Cambridge, 1794. Coleridge wrote
Act I; Southey, Acts II and III.
Poems, by Robert Lovell and Robert Southey, Bath, 1795.
Joan of Arc, An Epic Poem, Bristol, 1796.
Poems, Bristol, 1797, second edition, 1797.
Letters Written During a Short Residence in Spain and Portugal, Bristol, 1797,
rev. 1799, rev. 1808.
Poems, 1799.
Thalaba the Destroyer, 1801.
Madoc, 1805.
Metrical Tales and Other Poems, 1805.
Letters From England by Don Manuel Alvarez Espriella, 1807, reprint, ed
J. Simmons, 1951.
The Curse of Kehama, 1810.
History of Brazil, vol. 1, 1810, vol. 2, 1817, vol. 3, 1819.
Omniana, or Horae Otiosiores, 2 vols, 1812, [With Coleridge], ed R. Gittings,
1969.
The Origin, Nature and Object of the New System of Education, 1812, reprint,
1972.
An Exposure of the Misrepresentations and Calumnies in Mr Marsh's Review of

Sir George Barlow's administration at Madras, by the relatives of Sir George Barlow, 1813.

The Life of Nelson, 2 vols, 1813, many reprints, ed G. Callender, 1922, and E. H. R. Harvey, 1953.

Roderick, the Last of the Goths, 1814.

Odes To His Royal Highness the Prince Regent, His Imperial Majesty the Emperor of Russia, And His Majesty the King of Prussia, 1814.

Carmen Triumphale, For the Commencement of the Year 1814, 1814.

The Minor Poems of Robert Southey, 3 vols, reprints with some revision *Poems*, 1797, 1799, and *Metrical Tales*, 1805.

The Poet's Pilgrimage to Waterloo, 1816.

The Lay of the Laureate. Carmen Nuptiale, 1816.

Wat Tyler: A Dramatic Poem, 1817.

A Letter to William Smith, Esq. M.P., 1817.

The Life of Wesley; And the Rise and Progress of Methodism, 2 vols, 1820, many reprints, ed M. H. FitzGerald, Oxford, 1925.

A Vision of Judgment, 1821, ed R. Ellis Roberts, 1932.

The Expedition of Orsua; And the Crimes of Aguirre, 1821, reprinted from *Edinburgh Annual Register*, vol. 3.

The History of the Peninsular War, vol. 1, 1823, vol. 2, 1827, vol. 3, 1832.

The Book of the Church, 2 vols, 1824.

A Tale of Paraguay, 1825.

Vindiciae Ecclesiae Anglicanae, 1826.

All for Love; and The Pilgrim to Compostella, 1829.

Sir Thomas More; Or, Colloquies on the Progress and Prospects of Society, 2 vols, 1829.

Essays, Moral and Political, 2 vols, 1832.

Lives of the British Admirals, vols 1–2, 1833, vol. 3, 1834, vol. 4, 1837, reprinted as *English Seamen*, ed D. Hannay, 1895, 1904.

Letter to John Murray, Esq. 'Touching' Lord Nugent, 1833.

The Doctor, vols 1–2, 1834, vol. 3, 1836, vol. 4, 1837, vol. 5, 1838, vols 6–7, 1847, a one-volume edition, 1865, a one-volume selection ed M. H. FitzGerald, 1930.

The Life of the Reverend Andrew Bell, 3 vols, 1844, vols 2–3 by C. C. Southey.

Oliver Newman: A New-England Tale (Unfinished); With Other Poetical Remains, 1845.

Robin Hood: A Fragment, by the late Robert Southey and Caroline Southey, Edinburgh, 1847.

Common-Place Book, ed J. W. Warter, 4 vols, 1849–51.

Journal of a Tour in the Netherlands in the Autumn of 1815, Boston, 1902, ed W. R. Nicoll, 1903.

Journal of a Tour in Scotland in 1819, ed C. H. Herford, 1929.

Journals of a Residence in Portugal, 1800–1801 and a Visit to France, 1838, ed Adolfo Cabral, Oxford, 1960.

Editions and Translations

On the French Revolution, by Mr Necker, 1797, vol. 2 tr. by Southey.
The Annual Anthology, 2 vols, 1799–1800, Southey edited and contributed.
The Works of Thomas Chatterton, 3 vols, 1803, ed by Southey and Joseph Cottle.
Amadis of Gaul, by Vasco Lobeira, 4 vols, 1803, tr. by Southey.
The Remains of Henry Kirke White: With an Account of His Life, 1807.
Palmerin of England, by Francisco de Moraes, 4 vols, 1807, Munday's tr. corrected by Southey.
Specimens of the Later English Poets, 3 vols, 1807.
Chronicle of the Cid, 1808, ed with introduction by V. S. Pritchett, New York: Limited Editions Club, 1958.
The Geographical, Natural, and Civil History of Chili, by J. Ignatius Molina. 2 vols, 1809, annotated by Southey.
The Byrth, Lyf, and Actes of King Arthur, 2 vols, 1817.
The Pilgrim's Progress, With a Life of John Bunyan, 1830.
Attempts in Verse, by John Jones, an Old Servant: With . . . An Introductory Essay on the Lives and Works of Our Uneducated Poets, 1831, reprint of biographies by J. S. Childers, Oxford, 1925.
Select Works of the British Poets, From Chaucer to Jonson, With Biographical Sketches, 1831.
Horae Lyricae. Poems . . . By Isaac Watts. With a Memoir of the Author, 1834.
The Works of William Cowper . . . With a Life of the Author, 15 vols, 1835–7.
The Poetical Works of Southey, collected by himself, 10 vols, 1837–8, many reprints.
Poetical Works With a Memoir of the Author, H. T. Tuckerman, 10 vols, Boston, 1860, many reprints. Contains some posthumously published poems.
Poems of Robert Southey, ed M. H. FitzGerald, Oxford, 1909. Best selection.
Select Prose of Robert Southey, ed Jacob Zeitlin, New York, 1916.

Letters

The Life and Correspondence of the Late Robert Southey, ed C. C. Southey, 6 vols, 1849–50.
Selections from the Letters of Robert Southey, ed J. W. Warter, 4 vols, London, 1856.
The Correspondence of Robert Southey with Caroline Bowles, ed Edward Dowden. Dublin, 1881.
Letters of Robert Southey: A Selection, ed M. H. FitzGerald, Oxford (World's Classics), 1912. Best selection.
New Letters of Robert Southey, ed Kenneth Curry, 2 vols, New York, 1965.

Contains biographical sketches of Southey's friends and family as well as bibliographical footnotes identifying additions to the canon of Southey's writings.

Periodical Contributions

Southey contributed to the *Monthly Magazine*, 1796–1800; *Critical Review*, 1798–1803; *Annual Review*, 1802–8; *Athenaeum*, 1807–9; *Quarterly Review*, 1809–39; *Foreign Quarterly Review*, 1827; *Foreign Review*, 1828–30. Southey wrote the 'History of the Year' for the *Edinburgh Annual Register*, 1808–11 (published 1810–13) as well as contributing a few essays and poems. He also contributed poems to the *Morning Post*, 1798–9; 1801–3; occasional poems and letters to the *Courier*. Southey also wrote Spanish and Portuguese literary biographies for the *General Biography* (*New Letters*, vol. 1, 403*n* lists these). Occasional poems also appeared in the literary annuals.

Biographical and Critical Studies: Books and Articles

Cottle, Joseph, *Reminiscences of Samuel Taylor Coleridge and Robert Southey*, 1847. Entertaining but not always trustworthy anecdotes.

Dowden, Edward, *Southey*, English Men of Letters Series, 1879.

Pfandl, Ludwig, 'Robert Southey und Spanien,' *Revue hispanique*, 1913. Thorough treatment of all Southey's writings dealing with Spain and Spanish literature.

Haller, William, *The Early Life of Robert Southey*, 1917. The most thorough study of Southey's life and works until 1803.

Beer, M., *A History of British Socialism*, 1919.

Brinton, Crane, *The Political Ideas of the English Romanticists*, 1926.

Walter, F., *La Littérature portugaise en Angleterre à l'époque romantique*, Paris, 1927.

Wright, H. G., 'Southey's Relations with Finland and Scandinavia,' *Modern Language Review*, 1932. Authoritative article on Southey's knowledge of Scandinavian history and literature.

Hoadley, F. T., 'The Controversy over Southey's *Wat Tyler*,' *Studies in Philology*, 1941. Full treatment of the controversy and various printings of *Wat Tyler*.

Sousa Leão, J. de, 'Southey and Brazil,' *Modern Language Review*, 1943.

Sousa Leão, J. de, 'Robert Southey,' *Revista do Instituto Histórico e Geográfico Brasileiro*, 1943.

Curry, Kenneth, 'Southey's *Madoc*: the Manuscript of 1794,' *Philological Quarterly*, 1943. Gives full text of first attempt at *Madoc* – 2 1/2 books.

Baughman, R., 'Southey the Schoolboy,' *Huntington Library Quarterly*, 1944. Good account of Southey's life at Westminster School based on nine letters to Charles Collins.

Simmons, Jack, *Southey*, 1945, the standard biography. Perceptive, appreciative, and suitable for both the general reader and the scholar.

Schilling, B. N., *Human Dignity and the Great Victorians*, New York, 1946, ch. 4. Southey's ideas anticipate Morris, Kingsley, and Carlyle.

Bernbaum, Ernest, *Guide Through the Romantic Movement*, second edition, New York, 1949. Best short guide for introductory study.

Whalley, George, 'The Bristol Library Borrowings of Southey and Coleridge 1793–98,' *Library*, 1949.

Keynes, Geoffrey, *Blake Studies*, 1949. Full details of the Southey-Blake relationship.

Hopkins, Kenneth, *The Poets Laureate*, 1954. Good chapter on Southey as Laureate.

Anson, P. F., *The Call of the Cloister*, 1956.

Williams, Raymond, *Culture and Society: 1780–1950*, 1958.

Cabral, Adolfo, *Southey e Portugal*, Lisbon, 1959. Full discussion of Southey's Portuguese residence and writings on Portuguese history and literature. Written in Portuguese.

Carnall, Geoffrey, *Robert Southey and His Age: The Development of a Conservative Mind*, Oxford, 1960. A thorough and superb scholarly work. Contains best discussion of Southey's religious beliefs as well as of his political views.

Curry, Kenneth, 'The Library of Robert Southey,' *Studies in Honor of John C. Hodges and Alwin Thaler*, (*Tennessee Studies in Literature*, special number) 1961.

Carnall, Geoffrey, *Robert Southey*, British Council pamphlet, 1964.

Raimond, Jean, *Robert Southey: L'homme et son temps*; *L'oeuvre et le rôle*, Paris, 1968. Fullest discussion of every aspect of Southey's works.

Morgan, P. F., 'Southey's Poetry,' *Tennessee Studies in Literature*, 1971. Discusses Southey as a critic of poetry.

Madden, Lionel, ed., *Robert Southey: The Critical Heritage*, 1972. Useful reprint of reviews and comments upon Southey from 1794 to 1879.

Index

Index

Index

Index

Southey, Robert–*cont.*
and *Prospects of Society*, 53, 58, 73, 77, 82–9, 103, 176, 180; *Common-Place Book*, 103, 114, 116–17, 137, 180; 'Cornelius Agrippa,' 147; Cowper (William), *Works . . . With a Life of the Author*, 57, 74, 97–100, 136, 181; 'The Cross Roads,' 148; *Curse of Kehama*, 37, 45, 158, 162–7, 179; 'Death of Wallace,' 155; 'Destruction of Jerusalem,' 155; 'Devil's Walk,' 148; *The Doctor*, 51, 73, 103, 117–22, 180; 'Epistle to Allan Cunningham,' 173; *Essays Moral and Political*, 53, 135, 180; *Expedition of Orsua*, 180; 'Fair be thy fortunes,' 144; *Fall of Robespierre*, 26, 179; *Flagellant*, 10; 'God's Judgement on a Wicked Bishop,' 35, 144, 146; 'History,' 155; *History of Brazil*, 73, 125–7, 179; *History of the Peninsular War*, 73, 90, 123–5, 180; 'Holly Tree,' 35, 144, 153; 'Inchcape Rock,' 146, 149; 'Inscription for the Apartment in Chepstow Castle,' 151; 'Inscriptions,' 156–7; *Joan of Arc*, 19, 26, 34, 73, 141–3, 179; Jones (John), *Attempts in Verse: . . . Essay on the Lives and Works of Our Uneducated Poets*, 102, 136, 181; *Journal of a Residence in Portugal 1800–1801 and a Visit to France 1838*, 114, 180; *Journal of a Tour in the Netherlands in the Autumn of 1815*, 114, 180; *Journal of a Tour in Scotland in 1819*, 114–16, 180; 'King Henry and the Hermit of Dreux,' 155; *Lay of the Laureate*, 180; *Letter to William Smith. Esq. M. P.*, 55, 180; *Letters from England by Don Manuel Alvarez Espriella*, 46, 73, 77–82, 103, 176, 179; *Letters Written During a Short Residence in Spain and Portugal*, 31–2, 47, 73, 143, 179; *Life of John Wesley*, 57, 96–7, 130, 180; *Life of Nelson*, 50,

73, 93–6, 130, 176, 180; *Lives of the British Admirals*, 57, 180; 'Lord William,' 148; 'Love Elegies of Abel Shufflebottom,' 146; 'Lucretia,' 155; *Madoc*, 34, 158, 160–2, 179; Malory, Thomas, *see Morte D'Arthur*; 'Mary, the Maid of the Inn,' 148, 151; *Metrical Tales*, 144, 179; *Morte D'Arthur*, 135, 181; 'My days among the dead are past,' 153–4; 'Ode Written During the War With America,' 171–2; *Odes* (1816), 180; 'Old Woman of Berkeley,' 146; *Omniana*, 64, 179; *Palmerin of England*, 47, 74, 136, 181; 'Pauper's Funeral,' 143; 'Pious Painter,' 147; *Poems* (1795), 24, 73, 179; *Poems* (1797), 143, 149, 156, 157, 179; *Poems* (1799), 179; *Poet's Pilgrimage to Waterloo*, 11, 153, 180; 'Queen Mary's Christening,' 173; 'Queen Orraca and the Five Martyrs of Morocco,' 149; 'Recollections of a Day's Journey in Spain,' 153; 'Retrospect,' 4, 141; *Roderick*, 45, 158, 167–70, 180; 'Roprecht the Robber,' 149, 173; 'Ruined Cottage,' 150; 'St Antidius, the Pope and the Devil,' 147; 'St Michael's Chair,' 149; *Select Works of the British Poets, From Chaucer to Jonson*, 57, 135–6; *Sir Thomas More; Or Colloquies on the Progress and Prospects of Society*, *see Colloquies*; 'Soldier's Wife,' 143, 151; *Specimens of the Later English Poets*, 136, 181; *A Tale of Paraguay*, 180; *Thalaba the Destroyer*, 35, 37, 40, 54, 149, 158, 159–60, 179; 'The Three Bears,' 51, 154; 'To Charles Lamb on the Reviewal of His Album Verses in the *Literary Gazette*,' 67, 153; 'To the Evening Rainbow,' 144; 'To a Goose,' 145, 146; 'Triumph of[Woman,' 157; 'The Victory,' 155; *Vision of Judgment*, 51, 54, 69, 151, 172–3,

Southey

From this account of his life and writing, Robert Southey (1774-1843) emerges as a professional man of letters, who travelled widely and was in touch with the changing currents of his time.

Southey first made his reputation, when a very young man, as a poet and he is remembered now primarily for his poetry. In this book Southey is shown to be a writer who excelled in many other genres as well. His *Life of Nelson*, for example, is a biography in book form, he is the author of social and political criticism in his *Colloquies* and reviews for the *Quarterly Review*, of history in his *Brazil*, *Peninsular War* and *Book of the Church*, and of fiction in *The Doctor*. The many aspects of Southey's writing and all his major works are discussed here.

Examination of Southey's life and correspondence reveals an attractive and humane personality, at ease among his books, his family and a wide and impressive range of friends, including Wordsworth, Coleridge, Lamb, Landor and Scott. In addition to highlighting Southey's importance in his own age, the book, particularly in the discussion of the prose, points out his awareness of many aspects of life which cause concern to modern man, including the human loss brought about by industrialization and urbanization.